Application Building with Spec 2.0

K. De Hondt, S. Ducasse with S. Jordan Montaño and E. Lorenzano

October 26, 2024

Copyright © 2024 by K. De Hondt, S. Ducasse with S. Jordan Montaño and E. Lorenzano.

The contents of this book are protected under the Creative Commons Attribution-NonCommercial-NoDerivs CC BY-NC-ND
You are free to:

Share — copy and redistribute the material in any medium or format

The licensor cannot revoke these freedoms as long as you follow the license terms. Under the following conditions:

Attribution. — You must give appropriate credit, provide a link to the license, and indicate if changes were made. You may do so in any reasonable manner, but not in any way that suggests the licensor endorses you or your use.

NonCommercial. — You may not use the material for commercial purposes.

NoDerivatives. — If you remix, transform, or build upon the material, you may not distribute the modified material.

No additional restrictions. — You may not apply legal terms or technological measures that legally restrict others from doing anything the license permits.

https://creativecommons.org/licenses/by-nc-nd/4.0/legalcode

Any of the above conditions can be waived if you get permission from the copyright holder. Nothing in this license impairs or restricts the author's moral rights.

Keepers of the lighthouse
Édition : BoD · Books on Demand GmbH, In de Tarpen 42,
22848 Norderstedt (Allemagne)
Impression : Libri Plureos GmbH, Friedensallee 273,
22763 Hamburg (Allemagne)
ISBN : 978-2-3224-7871-2
Dépôt légal : 10/2024

Layout and typography based on the sbabook LaTeX class by Damien Pollet.

Contents

1	**Introduction**		**1**
1.1	Reuse of logic		1
1.2	Spec 2.0		3
1.3	Code		5
1.4	Acknowledgements		5

I	**All Spec in One Example**		
2	**A 10 min small example**		**9**
2.1	A customer satisfaction UI		9
2.2	Create the class of the UI		10
2.3	Instantiate and configure subpresenters		10
2.4	Define a title and window size, open and close the UI		13
2.5	Conclusion		14
3	**Most of Spec in one example**		**15**
3.1	Application		15
3.2	A basic film model		15
3.3	List of films		17
3.4	Filling up the film list		18
3.5	Opening presenters via the application		19
3.6	Improving the window		19
3.7	An application manages icons		20
3.8	FilmPresenter		20
3.9	Better looking FilmPresenter		22
3.10	Opening FilmPresenter in a modal dialog		24
3.11	Customizing the modal dialog		24
3.12	Invoking a presenter		25
3.13	Embedding a FilmPresenter into the FilmListPresenter		26
3.14	Define component communication		27
3.15	Testing your application UI		28
3.16	Adding more tests		30
3.17	Changing layout		31

3.18	Using transmissions	33
3.19	Styling the application	34
3.20	Conclusion	36

II Spec Essentials

4 Spec core in a nutshell — 39
4.1	Spec architecture overview	39
4.2	Spec core architecture overview	40
4.3	Presenters	41
4.4	Application	41
4.5	Application configuration	42
4.6	Layouts	43
4.7	Styles and stylesheets	45
4.8	Navigation between presenters	45
4.9	Conclusion	46

5 Testing Spec applications — 47
5.1	Testing presenters	47
5.2	Spec user example	49
5.3	Tests	53
5.4	Testing your application	58
5.5	Known limitations and conclusion	59

6 The dual aspects of presenters: Domain and interaction model — 61
6.1	About presenters on a model	61
6.2	Example with SpPresenter	62
6.3	SpPresenter vs. SpPresenterWithModel	63
6.4	Example with SpPresenterWithModel	63
6.5	User interface building: a model of UI presentation	65
6.6	The *initializePresenters* method	66
6.7	The *connectPresenters* method	67
6.8	The *defaultLayout* method	68
6.9	Conclusion	68

7 Reuse and composition at work — 69
7.1	First requirements	69
7.2	Creating a basic UI to be reused as a widget	70
7.3	Supporting reuse	71
7.4	Combining two basic presenters into a reusable UI	72
7.5	Live inspection of the widgets	74
7.6	Writing tests	74
7.7	Managing three widgets and their interactions	75
7.8	Having different layouts	78

Contents

7.9	Enhancing our API	78
7.10	Changing the layout of a reused widget	79
7.11	Changing layouts	81
7.12	Considerations about a public configuration API	81
7.13	New versus old patterns	82
7.14	Conclusion	83

8 Lists, tables and trees — 85

8.1	Lists	85
8.2	Controlling item display	85
8.3	Decorating elements	87
8.4	About single/multiple selection	87
8.5	Drag and drop	88
8.6	Activation clicks	89
8.7	Filtering lists	89
8.8	Selectable filtering lists	90
8.9	Component lists	91
8.10	Trees	92
8.11	Tables	94
8.12	First table	94
8.13	Sorting headers	95
8.14	Editable tables	96
8.15	Tree tables	97
8.16	Conclusion	99

9 Managing windows — 101

9.1	A working example	101
9.2	Opening a window or a dialog box	102
9.3	Preventing window close	104
9.4	Acting on window close	104
9.5	Window size and decoration	105
9.6	Getting values from a dialog window	108
9.7	Little modal dialog presenters	109
9.8	Placing a presenter inside a dialog window	110
9.9	Setting keyboard focus	111
9.10	Acting on window opening	111
9.11	Conclusion	113

10 Layouts — 115

10.1	Basic principle reminder	115
10.2	A running example	116
10.3	BoxLayout (SpBoxLayout and SpBoxConstraints)	116
10.4	Box layout alignment	119
10.5	Box alignment example	119

10.6	Alignment in horizontal box layout	122
10.7	A more advanced layout	123
10.8	Example setup for layout reuse	126
10.9	Opening with a layout	126
10.10	Better design	127
10.11	Specifying a layout when reusing a presenter	127
10.12	Alternative to declare subcomponent layout choice	129
10.13	Dynamically changing a layout	129
10.14	Grid layout (SpGridLayout)	130
10.15	Paned layout (SpPanedLayout)	132
10.16	Overlay layout (SpOverlayLayout)	133
10.17	Conclusion	136

11 Dynamic presenters — 137

11.1	Layouts as simple as objects	137
11.2	Dynamic button adder	140
11.3	Defining add/remove buttons	141
11.4	Building a little dynamic browser	142
11.5	Placing elements visually	144
11.6	Connecting the flow	145
11.7	Toggling Edit/Read-only mode	146
11.8	About layout recalculation	147
11.9	Conclusion	147

12 A Concrete Case: A Mail Application — 149

12.1	The models	150
12.2	Email	150
12.3	MailFolder	152
12.4	MailAccount	153
12.5	The presenters	155
12.6	The `EmailPresenter`	156
12.7	The `NoEmailPresenter`	157
12.8	The `MailReaderPresenter`	158
12.9	The `MailAccountPresenter`	159
12.10	The `MailClientPresenter`	161
12.11	First full application	163
12.12	Conclusion	164

13 Menubar, Toolbar, Status Bar, and Context Menus — 165

13.1	Adding a menubar to a window	165
13.2	Implementing message menu commands	167
13.3	Installing shortcuts	169
13.4	Defining actions	169
13.5	Adding a toolbar to a window	171

13.6	Supporting enablement	173
13.7	Adding a status bar to a window	174
13.8	Adding a context menu to a presenter	178
13.9	Enabling blocks	180
13.10	Conclusion	182

14 Using transmissions and ports — 183

14.1	What are transmissions?	183
14.2	A simple example	184
14.3	Basic transmission	185
14.4	Transforming a transmitted object	186
14.5	Acting on a transmission without input port	187
14.6	Acting after a transmission	188
14.7	Available ports	189
14.8	Ports and nesting presenters	190
14.9	A more advanced example	190
14.10	Another variation	191
14.11	Conclusion	192

15 Styling applications — 193

15.1	In a nutshell	193
15.2	How do styles work?	194
15.3	Stylesheets	194
15.4	Style declaration	195
15.5	Stylesheet examples	195
15.6	Anatomy of a style	196
15.7	Environment variables	197
15.8	Top-level changes	197
15.9	Defining an application and its style	198
15.10	Applying styles	199
15.11	Dynamically applying styles	201
15.12	Conclusion	203

16 Using Athens and Roassal in Spec — 205

16.1	Introduction	205
16.2	Direct integration of Athens with Spec	206
16.3	Roassal Spec integration	208
16.4	SpRoassalPresenter	209
16.5	Hello world in Athens via Morphic objects	210
16.6	Handling resizing	211
16.7	Using the morph with Spec	212
16.8	Conclusion	212

17 Customizing your Inspector — 213
- 17.1 Creating custom tabs — 213
- 17.2 Adding a tab with text — 214
- 17.3 A tab with a table — 215
- 17.4 Tab activation condition — 216
- 17.5 Adding a raw view of a specific element of the collection — 217
- 17.6 Removing the evaluator — 217
- 17.7 Adding Roassal charts — 218
- 17.8 Conclusion — 219

III Working with Commands

18 Commander: A powerful and simple command framework — 223
- 18.1 Commands — 223
- 18.2 Defining commands — 224
- 18.3 Adding a common superclass for the command classes — 224
- 18.4 Adding the main commands — 225
- 18.5 Adding placeholder commands — 227
- 18.6 Turning commands into menu items — 228
- 18.7 Using fillWith: — 229
- 18.8 Managing icons and shortcuts — 230
- 18.9 Managing a menubar — 231
- 18.10 Introducing groups — 233
- 18.11 Extending menus — 235
- 18.12 Declaring extension — 236
- 18.13 Managing a toolbar — 237
- 18.14 Conclusion — 241

CHAPTER 1

Introduction

Spec is a framework in Pharo for describing user interfaces. It allows for the construction of a wide variety of UIs; from small windows with a few buttons up to complex tools like a debugger. Indeed, multiple tools in Pharo are written in Spec, e.g., Iceberg the git manager, Change Sorter, Critics Browser, and the Pharo debugger. An important architectural decision is that Spec supports multiple backends (at the time of writing this book, GTK and Morphic are available).

1.1 Reuse of logic

The fundamental principle behind Spec is the reuse of user interface logic and its visual composition. User interfaces are built by reusing and composing existing user interfaces, and configuring them as needed. This principle starts from the most primitive elements of the UI: widgets such as buttons and labels are in themselves complete UIs that can be reused, configured, and opened in a window. These elements can be combined to form more complex UIs that again can be reused as part of a bigger UI, and so on. This is somewhat similar to how the different tiles on the cover of this book are combined. Smaller tiles configured with different colors or patterns join to form bigger rectangular shapes that are part of an even bigger floor design.

To allow such reuse, Spec was influenced by VisualWorks' and Dolphin Smalltalk's Model View Presenter (MVP) pattern. Spec recognizes the need for a Presenter class. A presenter represents the glue between a domain and widgets as well as the logic of interaction between the widgets composing the application.

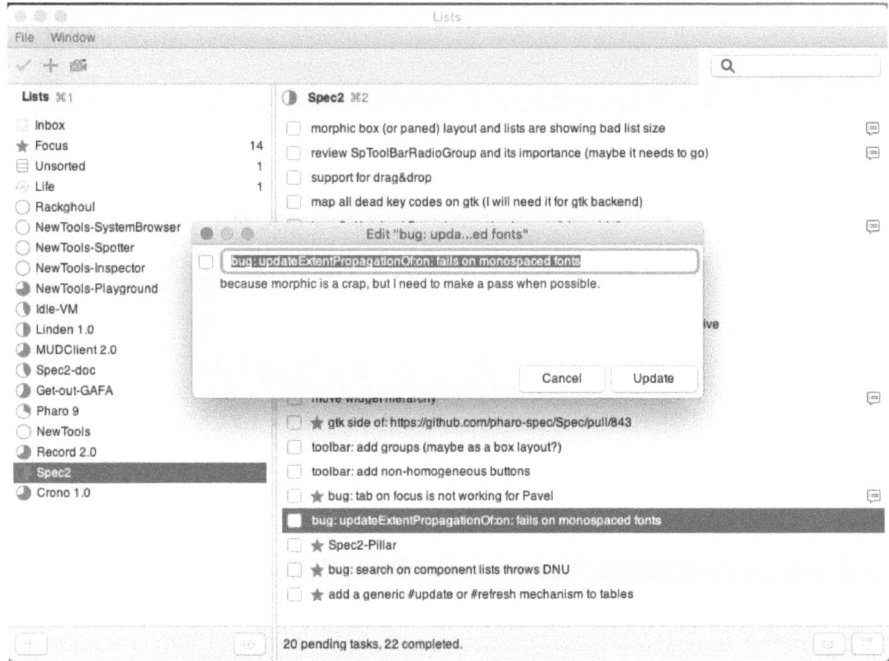

Figure 1-1 Spec supports multiple backends Morphic and GTK3.0.: Here we see GTK.

In Spec 1.0, this role was filled by the class ComposableModel and now, in Spec 2.0, the class is called SpPresenter. A presenter manages the *logic UI and the link between widgets and domain objects.* Fundamentally, when writing Spec code, developers do *not* come into contact with UI widgets. Instead, they program a Presenter that holds the UI logic (interactions, layout, ...) and talks to domain objects. When the UI is opened, this presenter instantiates the appropriate widgets. This being said, for developers, this distinction is not apparent and it feels as if the widgets are being programmed directly.

Spec is the standard GUI framework in Pharo and differs from Pharo's other GUI frameworks such as Morphic. It is restricted in that it only allows one to build user interfaces for applications that have typical GUI widgets such as buttons, lists, etc. It cannot be used as a general drawing framework, but you can integrate a canvas inside a Spec component.

For example, you can embed a Roassal visualization (see Figure 1-2), or you can extend Spec itself with additional native components.

Another example of integration is the NovaStelo project of Prof. E. Ito as shown in Figure 1-3. It shows that Spec can be used for the overall structure of the ap-

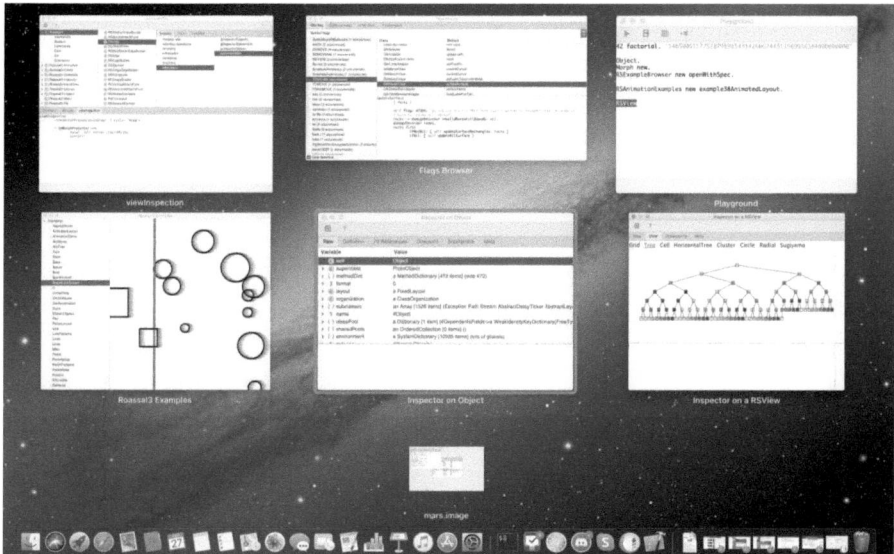

Figure 1-2 Roassal and Spec integration.

plication and embed specific elements. Figure 1-4 is the screenshot developed from a community member named Walehead.

1.2 Spec 2.0

Since Spec 2.0, different widget sets can be used to render your applications. At the time of writing this book, Spec can be rendered using either Morphic or GTK as a backend. Spec 2.0 represents a large iteration over Spec 1.0. Many enhancements have been introduced: the way user interface layouts are expressed, the API has been revisited, new widgets are supported, and integration with other projects, such as Commander, has been added.

Pharo's objective is to use Spec to build all its own GUIs. This ensures strong support of Spec over time and improves the standardization of Pharo's interfaces as well as their portability to new graphical systems. Using Spec 2.0 provides backend independence and logic reuse. This means that a UI written in Spec will be rendered on backends other than GTK and Morphic. As new backends become available, all applications written in Spec will be able to use them.

While this book uses previous Spec documentation as a foundation, the text has been almost completely rewritten to achieve higher quality. It covers re-

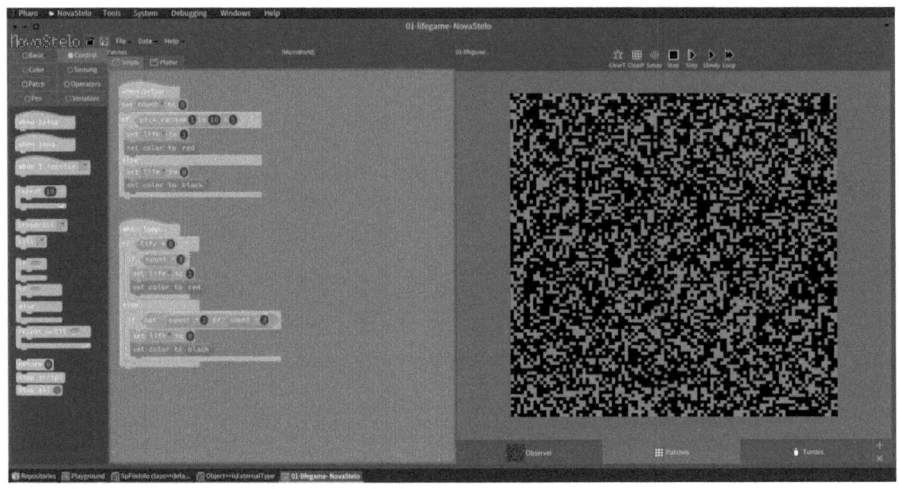

Figure 1-3   An integration of Morphic Native Widgets and Spec.

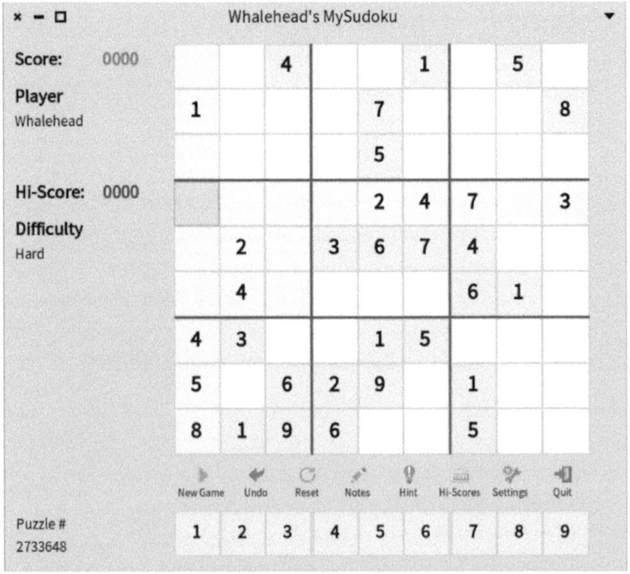

Figure 1-4   A suduko.

cent features. We hope that it will be useful to developers who write UIs in Pharo.

> **Note** This book focuses on Pharo 12. Earlier versions of Pharo come equipped with different versions of Spec, which may cause some code samples from this book to break. Nevertheless, the fundamental principles of UI development in Spec are the same.

1.3 Code

The code of all the examples in this book is stored at https://github.com/SquareBracketAssociates/CodeOfSpec20Book.

You can load the code by evaluating this code snippet:

```
Metacello new
    baseline: 'CodeOfSpec20Book';
    repository: 'github://SquareBracketAssociates/CodeOfSpec20Book/src';
    load
```

1.4 Acknowledgements

Even though due to the lack of manpower the fundraising campaign was not used, the authors would like to express their warm gratitude to the following people for their financial support: Masashi Fujita, Roch-Alexandre Nominé, Eiichiro Ito, sumim, Hilaire Fernandes, Dominique Dartois, Philippe Mougin, Pavel Krivanek, Michael L. Davis, Ewan Dawson, Luc Fabresse, David Bajger, Jörg Frank, Petter Egesund, Pierre Bulens, Tomohiro Oda, Sebastian Heidbrink, Alexandre Bergel, Jonas Skučas, and Mark Schwenk.

We want to thank I. Thomas for her chapter on the inspector, and R. De Villemeur for the chapter on Athens integration.

Finally, Stéphane Ducasse wants to thank Johan Fabry for his co-authoring of the first book on Spec 1.0. Without that first book, this one would not exist. He wants to thank Koen who happily jumped in as a co-author and tremendously improved the book. Thanks again Koen. It was a fun journey.

We want to thank ESUG and the Pharo Association for sponsoring this book. It was a real multiple year effort.

If you supported us and you are not on this list, please contact us or do a pull request.

Part I

All Spec in One Example

CHAPTER 2

A 10 min small example

We will construct a small but complete user interface. This will allow you to build basic user interfaces.

After completing this chapter you may read Chapter 7 about the reuse of Spec presenters, which is the key behind the power of Spec. With these two chapters, you should be able to construct Spec user interfaces as intended. You could use the rest of this book as reference material, but nonetheless, we recommend you to at least give a brief look at the other chapters as well.

2.1 A customer satisfaction UI

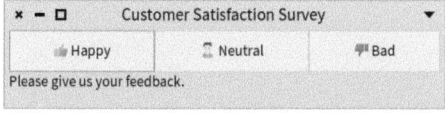

Figure 2-1 A screenshot of the customer satisfaction survey UI.

We construct a simple customer satisfaction survey UI, which allows a user to give feedback about a service by clicking on one of three buttons. This feedback should be recorded and processed, but that is outside of the scope of this example. Figure 2-1 shows a screenshot of the UI.

2.2 Create the class of the UI

All user interfaces in Spec are subclasses of `SpPresenter`, so the first step in creating the UI is subclassing that class:

```
SpPresenter << #CustomerSatisfactionPresenter
    slots: { #buttonHappy . #buttonNeutral . #buttonBad . #result};
    package: 'CodeOfSpec20Book'
```

The instance variables of the class hold the *presenters* the UI contains, the so-called *subpresenters*. In this case, we have three buttons and a text to show the result of the survey.

The methods of the class provide the initialization and configuration of the presenters, e.g., labels and actions, as well as the logic of their interaction. The basic design of our GUI, i.e., how the presenters are laid out, is defined by the class as well.

2.3 Instantiate and configure subpresenters

A subclass of `SpPresenter` has the responsibility to define the `initializePresenters` method, which instantiates and configures the presenters used in the user interface. We will discuss it piece by piece. Note that since this method may be a bit long we will split it into pieces that represent their intent.

Presenter creation

```
CustomerSatisfactionPresenter >> initializePresenters

    result := self newLabel.
    buttonHappy := self newButton.
    buttonNeutral := self newButton.
    buttonBad := self newButton.
```

`SpPresenter` defines messages for the creation of standard presenters: `newButton`, `newCheckBox`, `newDropList`, ... All of these are defined in the `scripting - widgets` protocol of the `SpTPresenterBuilder` trait. They are shortcuts to create presenters.

The following method shows how `newButton` is defined.

```
SpPresenter >> newButton

    ^ self instantiate: SpButtonPresenter
```

Note that the naming may be a bit confusing since we write `newButton` while it will create a button *presenter* and not a button *widget*, which Spec will take care

2.3 Instantiate and configure subpresenters

by itself. Spec provides `newButton` because it is easier to use than `newButton-Presenter`.

Do not call new to instantiate a presenter that is part of your UI. An alternative way to instantiate presenters is to use the message `instantiate:` with a presenter class as an argument. For example `result := self instantiate: SpLabelPresenter`. This allows one to instantiate standard and non-standard presenters.

Presenter configuration

The next step is configuring the buttons of our UI. The message `label:` sets the button label and the message `icon:` specifies the icon that will be displayed near the label.

```
CustomerSatisfactionPresenter >> initializePresenters

  ... continued ...
  result label: 'Please give us your feedback.'.
  buttonHappy
    label: 'Happy';
    icon: (self iconNamed: #thumbsUp).
  buttonNeutral
    label: 'Neutral';
    icon: (self iconNamed: #user).
  buttonBad
    label: 'Bad';
    icon: (self iconNamed: #thumbsDown)
```

The method `iconNamed:` of `SpPresenter` uses an icon provider to fetch the icon with the given name. You can browse the Spec icon provider by looking at `SpPharoThemeIconProvider`, which is a subclass of `SpIconProvider`. Each application is able to define its own icon provider by defining a subclass of `SpIconProvider`.

Presenter interaction logic

Now we define what will happen when the user presses a button. We define this in a separate method called `connectPresenters`:

```
CustomerSatisfactionPresenter >> connectPresenters

  buttonHappy action: [ result label: buttonHappy label ].
  buttonNeutral action: [ result label: buttonNeutral label ].
  buttonBad action: [ result label: buttonBad label ]
```

We use the message `action:` to specify the action that is performed when the button is clicked. In this case, we change the content of the result text to inform the user that the choice has been registered. Note that the message action: is part of the button API. In other situations, you will specify that when a given event occurs, some message should be sent to a subpresenter.

To summarize:

- Specialize `initializePresenters` to define and configure the presenters that are the elements of your UI.
- Specialize `connectPresenters` to connect those presenters together and specify their interaction.

Specifying the presenter layout

The presenters have been defined and configured, but their placement in the UI has not yet been specified. This is the role of the method `defaultLayout`.

```
CustomerSatisfactionPresenter >> defaultLayout

    ^ SpBoxLayout newTopToBottom
        add: (SpBoxLayout newLeftToRight
            add: buttonHappy;
            add: buttonNeutral;
            add: buttonBad;
            yourself);
        add: result;
        yourself
```

In this layout, we add two rows to the UI, one with the buttons and one with the result text. Defining presenter layout is a complex process with many different possible requirements, hence in this chapter we do not talk in detail about layout specification. For more information we refer to Chapter 10.

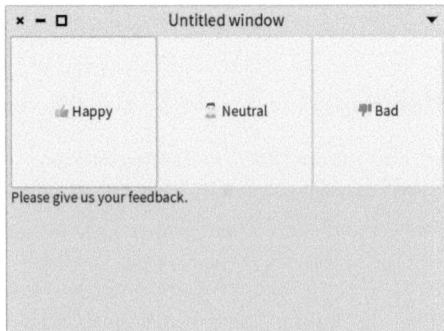

Figure 2-2 A first version of the customer satisfaction UI.

Once the method defaultLayout is defined, you can open your UI with CustomerSatisfactionPresenter new open. You should see a window similar to the one shown in Figure 2-2.

2.4 Define a title and window size, open and close the UI

To set the window title and the initial size of your presenter, you have to specialize the method initializeWindow: as follows:

```
CustomerSatisfactionPresenter >> initializeWindow: aWindowPresenter

    super initializeWindow: aWindowPresenter.
    aWindowPresenter
        title: 'Customer Satisfaction Survey';
        initialExtent: 400@100
```

You are free to use helper methods to return the title and extent of your presenter. When you reopen your presenter, and you click the "Happy" button, you should see the window shown in Fig. 2-3.

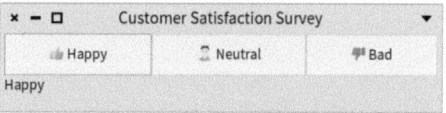

Figure 2-3 A final version of the customer satisfaction UI.

Sending the open message to a presenter will open a window and return an instance of SpWindowPresenter, which allows the window to be closed from code.

```
| ui |
ui := CustomerSatisfactionPresenter new open.
[ ... do a lot of stuff until the UI needs to be closed ...]
ui close
```

Note that to update the contents of your window once it is open, you have the method SpPresenter>>withWindowDo:, but we will discuss it later in this book. More information about managing windows, e.g., opening dialog boxes or setting the about text is present in Chapter 9.

This concludes our first example of a Spec user interface. In the next chapter, we continue with more examples on how to configure the different presenters that can be used in a user interface.

2.5 Conclusion

In this chapter, we have given you a small example of Spec user interfaces. We have shown you what the different steps are to build a user interface with Spec.

More examples of Spec user interfaces are found in the Pharo image. Since all Spec user interfaces are subclasses of `SpPresenter`, they are easy to find and each of them may serve as an example. Furthermore, experimentation with presenters and user interfaces is made easy because all presenters can be opened as standalone windows.

We recommend that you at least read Chapter 7 about reuse of Spec presenters, which is the key reason behind the power of Spec. This knowledge will help you in building UIs faster through better reuse, and also allow your own UIs to be reused.

CHAPTER 3

Most of Spec in one example

In this chapter, we will guide you through the building of a simple but nontrivial application to manage films as shown in Figure 3-1. We will show many aspects of Spec that we will revisit in depth in the rest of this book: the application, presenters, the separation between domain and presenter, layout, transmissions to connect widgets, and styles.

3.1 Application

Spec 2.0 introduces the concept of an application. An application is a small object responsible for keeping the state of your application. It manages, for example, the multiple windows that compose your application, and its backend (Morphic or GTK), and can hold properties shared by the presenters.

We start with the definition of the example application class:

```
SpApplication << #ImdbApp
    package: 'CodeOfSpec20Book'
```

3.2 A basic film model

Since we will manage films we define an ImdbFilm class as follows. It has a name, a year, and a director. We generate the companion accessors.

```
Object << #ImdbFilm
    slots: {#name . #year . #director};
    package: 'CodeOfSpec20Book'
```

Most of Spec in one example

Figure 3-1 Film app: reusing the same component to edit and browsing a film.

We need a way to store and query films. We could use Voyage (https://github.com/pharo-nosql/voyage) since it works without an external Mongo DB. But we want to keep it extremely simple. So let's define a singleton.

We define a *class* instance variable called `films`.

```
Object class << ImdbFilm class
    slots: { #films }
```

We define a method that lazy initializes the `films` variable to an ordered collection.

```
ImdbFilm class >> films

    ^ films ifNil: [ films := OrderedCollection new ]
```

And to finish we define a way to add a film to the list.

```
ImdbFilm class >> addFilm: aFilm

    films add: aFilm
```

Now we are ready to define a first presenter that manages a list of films.

16

3.3 List of films

We define a presenter to manage a list of films by introducing a new class named `ImdbFilmListPresenter` which inherits from `SpPresenter`. We add an instance variable named `filmList` that will hold an elementary list presenter.

```
SpPresenter << #ImdbFilmListPresenter
    slots: { #filmList };
    package: 'CodeOfSpec20Book'
```

We define how the information should be presented by defining a method named `defaultLayout`. We specify a simple vertical box layout with the `film-List` as the only element.

defaultLayout

```
ImdbFilmListPresenter >> defaultLayout

    ^ SpBoxLayout newTopToBottom
        add: filmList;
        yourself
```

When you do not define any other methods to represent layout, `defaultLayout` is the method that is invoked by Spec logic.

A presenter can have subpresenters. `ImdbFilmListPresenter` contains a table presenter and you will see later that:

1. a presenter can have multiple layouts
2. layouts can be defined dynamically

In Spec, layouts are dynamic by default and are expressed at the instance level. To allow backward compatibility, it is still possible to define a `defaultLayout` *class-side* method that returns a layout instead of using a `defaultLayout` instance-side method, but it is not the recommended way.

initializePresenters

So far, we have not initialized `filmList`.

The place to initialize the subpresenters is the method `initializePresenters` as shown below. There we define that `filmList` is a table with three columns. The message `newTable` instantiates a `SpTablePresenter`.

```
ImdbFilmListPresenter >> initializePresenters

    filmList := self newTable
        addColumn: (SpStringTableColumn title: 'Name'
```

```
        evaluated: #name);
    addColumn: (SpStringTableColumn title: 'Director'
        evaluated: #director);
    addColumn: (SpStringTableColumn title: 'Year'
        evaluated: #year);
    yourself
```

The following expression creates an instance of the film list presenter and opens it. You get the window shown in Figure 3-2.

```
ImdbFilmListPresenter new open
```

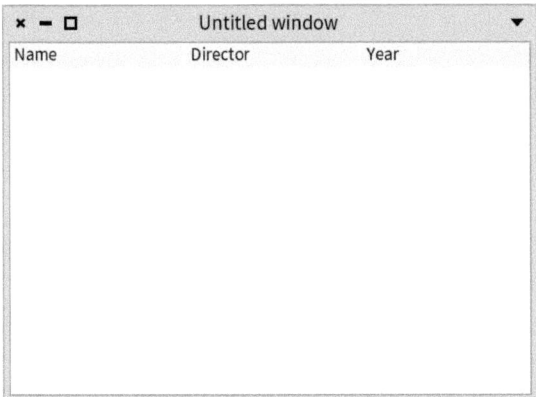

Figure 3-2 A layout and a simple `initializePresenters` showing an empty list of films.

3.4 Filling up the film list

We define the method `updatePresenter` which is automatically invoked after `initializePresenters`. It just queries the domain (`ImdbFilm`) to get the list of the recorded films and populates the internal table. Right now we do not have any film in the singleton so the list of films is empty.

```
ImdbFilmListPresenter >> updatePresenter

    filmList items: ImdbFilm films
```

If you want, just add a film and reopen the presenter. You should see the film on the list.

3.5 Opening presenters via the application

```
ImdbFilm addFilm: (ImdbFilm new
    name: 'E.T.';
    director: 'Steven Spielberg';
    year: '1982';
    yourself)
```

3.5 Opening presenters via the application

While directly creating a presenter is possible during development, a more canonical way to create a presenter is to ask the application using the message newPresenter: as follows.

```
| app |
app := ImdbApp new.
(app newPresenter: ImdbFilmListPresenter) open
```

The application is responsible for managing windows and other information, therefore it is important to use it to create presenters that compose the application.

3.6 Improving the window

A presenter can be embedded in another presenter as we will show later. It can also be placed within a window and this is what the message open does. Spec offers another hook, the method initializeWindow:, to specialize the information presented when a presenter is displayed within a window.

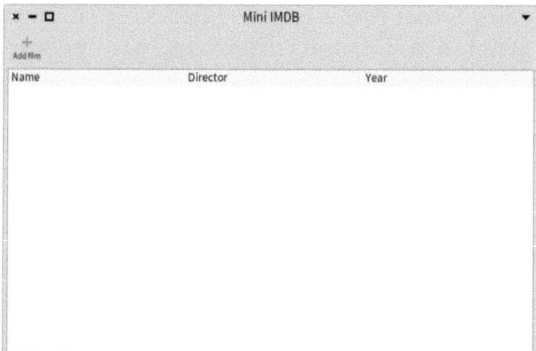

Figure 3-3 Film list presenter with a toolbar and a decorated window.

The method initializeWindow: allows you to define a title, a default size (message initialExtent:), and a toolbar.

19

```
ImdbFilmListPresenter >> initializeWindow: aWindowPresenter

    | addButton toolbar |
    addButton := self newToolbarButton
        label: 'Add film' ;
        icon: (self iconNamed: #smallAdd);
        action: [ self addFilm ];
        yourself.
    toolbar := self newToolbar
        add: addButton;
        yourself.
    aWindowPresenter
        title: 'Mini IMDB';
        initialExtent: 600@400;
        toolbar: toolbar
```

You should obtain the window with a toolbar as shown in Figure 3-3. To make sure that the Add film button does not raise an error, we trigger an addFilm method that is defined with no behavior. In fact, we will define a different presenter to be able to define a film.

```
ImdbFilmListPresenter >> addFilm

    "empty for now"
```

As we will see in Chapter 18, toolbars can be automatically created out of commands. We could have added the toolbar in that way to the filmList (e.g. using an instance variable) as part of the ImdbFilmListPresenter because the toolbar is also a presenter (similar to the table presenter or other predefined presenters). But doing it that way is less modular. Note also that the toolbar we created could be factored in a separate class to increase reuse too.

3.7 An application manages icons

What we can see from the definition of the method initializeWindow: is that an application manages icons with the message iconNamed:. Indeed, a presenter defines the iconNamed: message as a delegation to its application. In addition, your application can define its own icon set using the message iconProvider:.

3.8 FilmPresenter

We are ready to define a simple presenter to edit a film. We will use it to add a new film or simply display it. We create a new subclass of SpPresenter named

3.8 FilmPresenter

`ImdbFilmPresenter`. This class has three instance variables: `nameText`, `directorText`, and `yearNumber`.

```
SpPresenter << #ImdbFilmPresenter
    slots: { #nameText . #directorText . #yearNumber };
    package: 'CodeOfSpec20Book'
```

As we did previously, we define a default layout. This time we use a grid layout. With a grid layout, you can choose the position in the grid where your presenters will appear.

```
ImdbFilmPresenter >> defaultLayout

    ^ SpGridLayout new
        add: 'Name' at: 1@1; add: nameText at: 2@1;
        add: 'Director' at: 1@2; add: directorText at: 2@2;
        add: 'Year' at: 1@3; add: yearNumber at: 2@3;
        yourself
```

Note that it is not required to create the accessors for the presenter elements as we were forced to do in Spec 1.0. Here we only create getters because we will need them when creating the corresponding `ImbdFilm` instance.

```
ImdbFilmPresenter >> year

    ^ yearNumber text

ImdbFilmPresenter >> director

    ^ directorText text

ImdbFilmPresenter >> name

    ^ nameText text
```

For convenience, a `SpGridLayout` also comes with a builder that lets you add elements to the layout in the order they will appear. The previous layout definition can be rewritten as:

```
ImdbFilmPresenter >> defaultLayout

    ^ SpGridLayout build: [ :builder |
        builder
            add: 'Name'; add: nameText; nextRow;
            add: 'Director'; add: directorText; nextRow;
            add: 'Year'; add: yearNumber ]
```

Pay attention: do not add a `yourself` message here because you would return the class and not the layout instance.

Most of Spec in one example

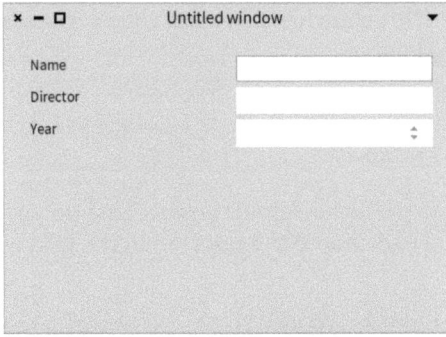

Figure 3-4 A single film presenter.

And as before, we define the method `initializePresenters` to initialize the variables to the corresponding elementary presenters. Here `nameText` and `directorText` are initialized to a text input, and `yearNumber` is a number input.

```
ImdbFilmPresenter >> initializePresenters

    nameText := self newTextInput.
    directorText := self newTextInput.
    yearNumber := self newNumberInput
        rangeMinimum: 1900 maximum: Year current year;
        yourself
```

Now we can try our little application with the following script and obtain a window similar to the one shown in Figure 3-4:

```
| app |
app := ImdbApp new.
(app newPresenter: ImdbFilmPresenter) open
```

3.9 Better looking FilmPresenter

We improve the look of the film presenter by specifying column behavior and setting window properties. As you can see, the form to present Film data has very large labels. Indeed, they take half of the form width. We can solve that by using non-homogenous columns and asking the second column to take the biggest possible width with `column:expand:`. See Figure 3-5.

3.9 Better looking FilmPresenter

```
ImdbFilmPresenter >> defaultLayout

  ^ SpGridLayout build: [ :builder |
      builder
        beColumnNotHomogeneous;
        column: 2 expand: true;
        add: 'Name'; add: nameText; nextRow;
        add: 'Director'; add: directorText; nextRow;
        add: 'Year'; add: yearNumber ]
```

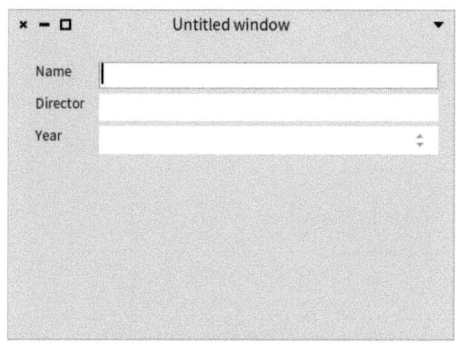

Figure 3-5   Using a non-homogenous grid layout.

Now we set the window properties by adding the following new `initializeWindow:` method. We get the situation shown in Figure 3-6.

```
ImdbFilmPresenter >> initializeWindow: aWindowPresenter

  aWindowPresenter
    title: 'Film';
    initialExtent: 400@250
```

Figure 3-6   Better window.

3.10 Opening FilmPresenter in a modal dialog

Instead of opening the film presenter in a separate window, we like to open it in a modal dialog window. The modal dialog blocks the user interface until the user confirms or cancels the dialog. A modal dialog has no window decorations and it cannot be moved.

While a window can be opened by sending `open` to an instance of a presenter class, a dialog can be opened by sending `openModal`.

```
| app |
app := ImdbApp new.
(app newPresenter: ImdbFilmPresenter) openModal
```

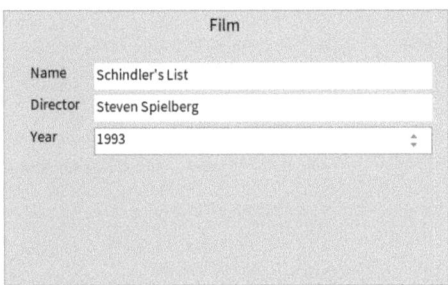

Figure 3-7 A modal dialog.

Figure 3-7 shows the result. Note that there are no UI components to close the dialog. Press the "Esc" key on the keyboard to close it.

3.11 Customizing the modal dialog

Spec lets us adapt the dialog window, for example, to add interaction buttons. We specialize the method `initializeDialogWindow:` to add two buttons that control the behavior of the application, as shown in Figure 3-8. We also center the dialog on screen by sending `centered` to the dialog presenter.

```
ImdbFilmPresenter >> initializeDialogWindow: aDialogPresenter

  aDialogPresenter centered.
  aDialogPresenter
    addButton: 'Cancel' do: [ :button | button close ];
    addButton: 'Save Film' do: [ :button | button beOk; close ].
```

Figure 3-8 Customizing the dialog window.

3.12 Invoking a presenter

We are ready to use the film presenter from within the film list presenter. We define the method `addFilm` in the class `ImdbFilmListPresenter`. When the user clicks on the button, we create a new film presenter that we associate with the current application.

We open the film presenter as a modal dialog using the message `openModal`. When the user presses the "Save Film" button, a new film is added to our little database and we update the list.

```
ImdbFilmListPresenter >> addFilm

  | dialog windowPresenter film |
  dialog := ImdbFilmPresenter newApplication: self application.
  windowPresenter := dialog openModal.
  windowPresenter isOk ifFalse: [ ^ self ].

  film := ImdbFilm new
    name: dialog name;
    director: dialog director;
    year: dialog yearNumber.
  ImdbFilm addFilm: film.
  self updatePresenter
```

Now we can open the `FilmListPresenter` and click on the `Add film` button. When the film data has been entered and the `Save Film` button has been clicked, you will see that the FilmListPresenter is updated with the added film, as shown in Figure 3-9.

```
app := ImdbApp new.
(app newPresenter: ImdbFilmListPresenter) open
```

Most of Spec in one example

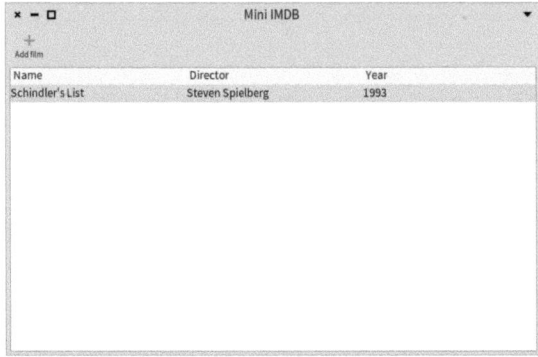

Figure 3-9 The refreshed film list.

3.13 Embedding a FilmPresenter into the FilmListPresenter

We have two main visual elements: a list of films and the film details. We can imagine that we would like to see the film details in the same container as the list, especially because a film description is larger than the list columns.

To achieve that, we add a new instance variable named `detail` to the class `ImdbFilmListPresenter`.

```
SpPresenter << #ImdbFilmListPresenter
    slots: { #filmList . #detail };
    package: 'CodeOfSpec20Book'
```

We redefine the default layout. We will show later that we can have different layouts.

```
ImdbFilmListPresenter >> defaultLayout

    ^ SpBoxLayout newTopToBottom
        add: filmList;
        add: detail;
        yourself
```

Since we are going to use this presenter in different places, we have to add a method to control whether it is editable or not:

```
ImdbFilmPresenter >> editable: aBoolean

    nameText editable: aBoolean.
    directorText editable: aBoolean.
    yearNumber editable: aBoolean
```

Now we improve the `initializePresenters` of `ImdbFilmListPresenter`.

- First we instantiate `ImdbFilmPresenter`.
- Second, we configure it as read-only by sending the `editable: false` message.
- Third, when an element of the list is selected, we should display the information in the detail presenter. While we can express this in the `initializePresenters` method, we prefer specifying it in the `connectPresenters` method. See Section 3.14.

```
ImdbFilmListPresenter >> initializePresenters

  filmList := self newTable
    addColumn: (SpStringTableColumn title: 'Name'
      evaluated: #name);
    addColumn: (SpStringTableColumn title: 'Director'
      evaluated: #director);
    addColumn: (SpStringTableColumn title: 'Year'
      evaluated: #year);
    yourself.
  detail := self instantiate: ImdbFilmPresenter.
  detail editable: false
```

3.14 Define component communication

We add a helper method named `setModel:` in class `ImdbFilmPresenter` to be able to pass a film and populate the presenter accordingly.

```
ImdbFilmPresenter >> setModel: aFilm

  aFilm
    ifNil: [
      nameText text: ''.
      directorText text: ''.
      yearNumber number: '' ]
    ifNotNil: [
      nameText text: aFilm name.
      directorText text: aFilm director.
      yearNumber number: aFilm year ]
```

It is important to check for a `nil` value, otherwise sending `name`, `director`, or `year` would fail. If the given `aFilm` argument is `nil`, we clear the three subpresenters.

Note that the method `setModel:` is needed only if you do not subclass from `SpPresenterWithModel`. If you subclass from `SpPresenter`, it is the only way to have the model initialized before the setup of the presenter, and avoid errors when opening the presenter.

Defining interactions between presenters is done in the `connectPresenters` method. We implement it to define that, when an element of the list is selected, we display the information in the detail presenter. It is worth taking some time to look at the `whenSelectionChangedDo:` method.

The `whenSelectionChangedDo:` method expects a block with at most one argument. The argument does not hold the selected item directly, but a more complex object that represents the selection. Indeed a selection is different in a single selection list and a multiple selection list. Therefore Spec defines the concept of selection mode under the form of subclasses of `SpAbstractSelectionMode`.

```
ImdbFilmListPresenter >> connectPresenters

filmList whenSelectionChangedDo: [ :selectedItemMode |
    detail setModel: selectedItemMode selectedItem ]
```

With `connectPresenters` in place, selecting an item in the list results in showing the details of the selected item, as shown in Figure 3-10.

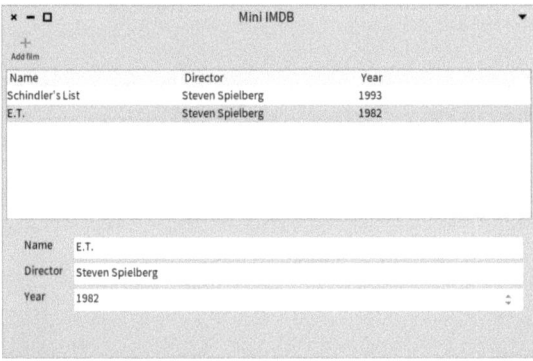

Figure 3-10 Embedding the film description in the list: selecting a list item populates the detailed visual component.

3.15 Testing your application UI

A strong property of Spec is that we can write tests to describe the interaction and the logic of a UI. Tests are so powerful to help us create nice designs and make sure that we can spot errors, that we will show that writing tests for a UI is not complex.

We define `ImdbFilmListPresenterTest` as a subclass of `TestCase`.

3.15 Testing your application UI

```
TestCase << #ImdbFilmListPresenterTest
  package: 'CodeOfSpec20Book'
```

```
ImdbFilmListPresenterTest >>
    testWhenSelectingOneFilmThenDetailIsUpdated

  | presenter detail |
  "Arrange"
  presenter := ImdbFilmListPresenter new.
  presenter open.
  detail := presenter detail.
  self assert: detail name isEmpty.

  "Act"
  presenter clickFilmAtIndex: 1.

  "Assert"
  self deny: detail name isEmpty.
  presenter delete
```

As you see, we will have to define two methods on `ImdbFilmListPresenter` to support proper testing: a getter for `detail` and an interaction method `clickFilmAtIndex:`. We categorize them in the `testing - support` protocol to indicate that they are only intended for testing purposes.

```
ImdbFilmListPresenter >> detail

  ^ detail
```

```
ImdbFilmListPresenter >> clickFilmAtIndex: anIndex

  filmList clickAtIndex: anIndex
```

This test is a bit poor because we do not explicitly test the value of the film's name in the `detail` presenter. We did this to keep the test setup simple, partly because `ImdbFilm` stores the current films globally. Singletons are ugly and they also make testing more complex.

We define three helper methods on `ImdbFilm` to reset the stored films and add the E.T. film.

```
ImdbFilm class >> reset

  films := OrderedCollection new
```

```
ImdbFilm class >> addET

  films add: self ET
```

```
ImdbFilm class >> ET

    ^ self new
        name: 'E.T.';
        director: 'Steven Spielberg';
        year: '1982';
        yourself
```

Now we can define the `setUp` method.

```
ImdbFilmListPresenterTest >> setUp

    super setUp.
    ImdbFilm reset.
    ImdbFilm addET
```

Now we update the test to keep the opened presenter in an instance variable. This allows us to define a `tearDown` method that always closes the presenter, no matter if the test succeeds or fails.

```
ImdbFilmListPresenterTest >>
      testWhenSelectingOneFilmThenDetailIsUpdated

    | detail |
    "Arrange"
    presenter := ImdbFilmListPresenter new.
    presenter open.
    detail := presenter detail.
    self assert: detail name isEmpty.

    "Act"
    presenter clickFilmAtIndex: 1.

    "Assert"
    self deny: detail name isEmpty
```

```
ImdbFilmListPresenterTest >> tearDown

    presenter ifNotNil: [ presenter delete ].
    super tearDown
```

3.16 Adding more tests

Tests are addictive because we can change programs and check that they still work and limit our stress. So we will write another one.

Let us add the following getter method to support our tests.

```
ImdbFilmListPresenter >> filmList

    ^ filmList
```

Let us test that a list has one film and that if we select a non-existent index, the name is cleared.

```
ImdbFilmListPresenterTest >> testNoSelectionClearsDetails

    | name |
    "Arrange"
    presenter := ImdbFilmListPresenter new.
    presenter open.

    "Act"
    presenter clickFilmAtIndex: 1.

    "Assert"
    name := presenter detail name.
    self deny: name isEmpty.
    self assert: presenter filmList listSize equals: 1.

    presenter clickFilmAtIndex: 2.
    self assert: presenter detail name equals: ''
```

Multiple selection is not supported. Therefore we test that `filmList` is configured for single selection. There is no `isSingleSelection` method, so instead of asserting single selection, we deny multiple selection.

```
ImdbFilmListPresenterTest >> testListIsSingleSelection

    presenter := ImdbFilmListPresenter new.
    presenter open.
    self deny: presenter filmList isMultipleSelection
```

What you see is that it is relatively simple to test that the interaction you specified actually works as expected.

3.17 Changing layout

With Spec, a presenter can have multiple layouts, even layouts that are created on the fly as we will see with dynamic layouts. We can decide which layout to use when opening a presenter. Let us illustrate that. Imagine that we prefer to have the list positioned below the film details, or just the list alone.

```
ImdbFilmListPresenter >> listBelowLayout

    ^ SpBoxLayout newTopToBottom
        add: detail;
        add: filmList;
        yourself
```

The following example shows that we can open ImdbFilmListPresenter with the layout listBelowLayout that we just defined. See Figure 3-11.

```
| app presenter |
app := ImdbApp new.
presenter := app newPresenter: ImdbFilmListPresenter.
presenter openWithLayout: presenter listBelowLayout.
```

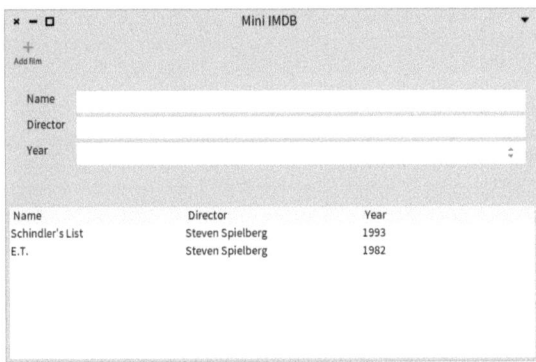

Figure 3-11 A presenter can have multiple layouts for its subpresenters.

We can also define a layout with a part of the subpresenters. Here listOnlyLayout only shows the list.

```
ImdbFilmListPresenter >> listOnlyLayout

    ^ SpBoxLayout newTopToBottom
        add: filmList;
        yourself
```

The following example shows that we can open ImdbFilmListPresenter with one layout and dynamically change it by another layout. In a playground, do not declare the temporary variables so that they are bound and kept in the playground.

```
app := ImdbApp new.
presenter := app newPresenter: ImdbFilmListPresenter.
presenter open
```

The presenter opens with the default layout. Now in the playground execute the following line.

```
presenter layout: presenter listOnlyLayout
```

Now you can see that the layout with only one list has been applied dynamically.

3.18 Using transmissions

Spec 2.0 introduces a nice concept to propagate selections from one presenter to another, thinking about the "flow" of information more than the implementation details of this propagation, which can change from presenter to presenter.

With transmissions, each presenter can define a set of output ports (ports to transmit information) and input ports (ports to receive information). Widget presenters already have defined the output/input ports you can use with them, but you can add your own ports to your presenters.

The easiest way to declare a transmission is by sending the `transmitTo:` message from one presenter to another. We can now change the `connectPresenters` method to use transmissions.

```
ImdbFilmListPresenter >> connectPresenters

    filmList transmitTo: detail
```

Here, `filmList` is a table that will transmit its selection to the `detail` presenter.

Let us explain a bit. `ImdbFilmPresenter` is a custom presenter. Spec does not know how to "fill" it with input data. We need to tell Spec that `ImdbFilmPresenter` model will be the input port and receive the input data. Therefore we need to define an input port as follows:

```
ImdbFilmPresenter >> inputModelPort

    ^ SpModelPort newPresenter: self
```
```
ImdbFilmPresenter >> defaultInputPort

    ^ self inputModelPort
```

Note that we could have inlined `inputModelPort`'s definition into the `defaultInputPort` definition.

The input data will be set by using the `setModel:` method we already defined on `ImdbFilmPresenter`. `SpModelPort` takes care of that.

Now you can open the application and see that it still behaves as expected.

```
| app |
app := ImdbApp new.
(app newPresenter: ImdbFilmListPresenter) open
```

3.19 Styling the application

Different UI components in an application can have different look and feels, for example to change the size or color of a font for a header. To support this, Spec introduces the concept of "styles" for components.

In Spec, an application defines a stylesheet (or a set of them). A stylesheet defines a set of "style classes" that can be assigned to presenter widgets. Defining a style class, however, works differently for each backend. While GTK accepts (mostly) regular CSS to style widgets, Morphic has its own subframework.

An application comes with a default configuration and a default stylesheet. If you do not need to style your application, there is no need to define them. In our example, we would like to define a `header` style to customize some labels. In Spec every presenter understands the message `addStyle:` that adds a tag (a CSS class) to the receiver.

To do so, you need to declare a stylesheet in a configuration. The configuration itself needs to be declared in your application. We will define a new presenter for the label and tag it with a specific CCS class using the message `addStyle:`. Our CCS class will be named `'customLabel'`.

First, we create the specific configuration for our application.

```
SpMorphicConfiguration << #ImdbConfiguration
    package: 'CodeOfSpec20Book'
```

Second, we use it in `ImdbApp`.

```
ImdbApp >> initialize

    super initialize.
    self
        useBackend: #Morphic
        with: ImdbConfiguration new
```

Then we can define our custom styles. The easiest way is to create a style from a String. Here we define that an element using the tag `customLabel` will have red text.

3.19 Styling the application

```
ImdbConfiguration >> customStyleSheet

  ^ '
.application [
  .customLabel [ Font { #color: #red } ] ]'
```

Pay attention not to forget the '.' in front of `application` and `customLabel`

We specialize the method `configure:` so that it includes the custom style as follows:

```
ImdbConfiguration >> configure: anApplication

  super configure: anApplication.
  self addStyleSheetFromString: self customStyleSheet
```

We are ready to use the tag for the label. Until now, Spec was creating a presenter for the label automatically, but it was not accessible by the developer. Therefore we have to add a label explicitly so that we can tag it with a CSS-like class. This is what the message `addStyle: 'customLabel'` below does.

We add a `nameLabel` instance variable to `ImdbFilmPresenter` to hold a label, and we initialize it in the method `initializePresenters` as follows:

```
ImdbFilmPresenter >> initializePresenters

  nameLabel := self newLabel
    label: 'Name';
    addStyle: 'customLabel';
    yourself.
  nameText := self newTextInput.
  directorText := self newTextInput.
  yearNumber := self newNumberInput
    rangeMinimum: 1900 maximum: Year current year;
    yourself
```

Then we update the layout to use the newly defined label presenter.

```
ImdbFilmPresenter >> defaultLayout

  ^ SpGridLayout build: [ :builder |
    builder
      beColumnNotHomogeneous;
      column: 2 withConstraints: #beExpand;
      add: nameLabel; add: nameText; nextRow;
      add: 'Director'; add: directorText; nextRow;
      add: 'Year'; add: yearNumber ]
```

Now we see that the name label of a film detail has been styled, as shown in Figure 3-12.

35

Figure 3-12 Styled film name label.

3.20 Conclusion

We saw that with Spec the developer defines how a visual element (a presenter) is composed of other visual elements. Such a presenter has the responsibility to describe the interaction with other presenters, but also with the domain objects. It has also the responsibility to describe its visual aspects.

Part II

Spec Essentials

CHAPTER 4

Spec core in a nutshell

Spec is Pharo's user interface framework. It provides the building blocks for constructing UIs, from simple windows to complex tools like browsers and debuggers. With Spec, developers can capture the layout and the interactions between the elements that compose a UI. For example, a developer can express that a tool has two components: a list on the left and a component displaying information on the right. Clicking on an item in the list will display detailed information about the selected item. In addition, Spec supports the reuse of the UI interaction logic.

Spec is the foundation of most tools in Pharo, such as the inspector, Spotter, the Pharo debugger, Iceberg, etc. In this short chapter, we place the key architectural elements of Spec in context.

4.1 Spec architecture overview

Figure 4-1 presents the general architecture of Spec. Basically, Spec is built around 5 concepts that we will describe in subsequent sections. The most important concepts are *presenter*, *layout*, and *application*.

A *presenter* represents the UI element logic and it is also the connection with the domain. The Application is also a place to be in contact with domain objects but generally, it handles application-specific resources (icons, windows,...).

Based on presenters and layouts, Spec builds the actual UI. Internally, it uses adapters that are specific to each widget and per backend. This way presenters are agnostic about backends and are reusable across them.

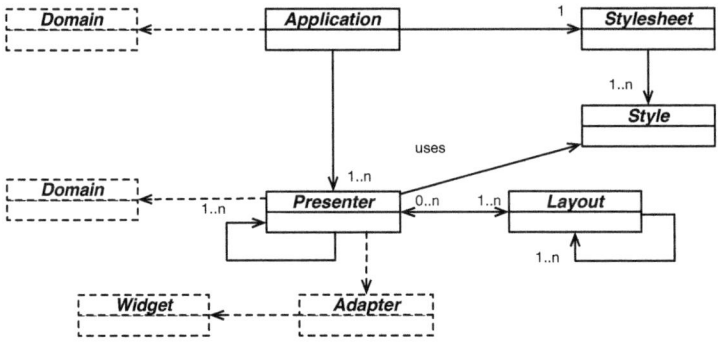

Figure 4-1 Architecture of Spec.

4.2 Spec core architecture overview

Spec core is composed of the following elements:

- **Application.** An application is composed of multiple presenters and a stylesheet.
- **Presenters.** A presenter is a unit of interactive behavior. It is connected to domain objects and other presenters. Its visual representation is defined via at least one layout.
- **Layout.** A layout describes the positions of elements and it can be recursive.
- **Stylesheet and styles.** A stylesheet is composed of styles that describe visual properties such as fonts, colors, ...

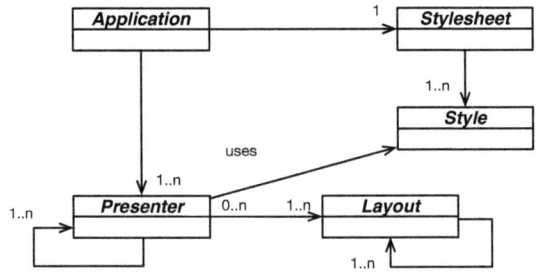

Figure 4-2 Presenter, Application, Layout, and Style of Spec.

We detail each of the main elements.

4.3 Presenters

A Spec presenter (an instance of a `SpPresenter` subclass), is an essential part of the Spec framework. It represents the logic of a UI element. It can define the behavior of a simple UI widget such as a button, as well as of a complex UI widget composed by many other presenters (either simple or complex). To build your user interface, you compose presenters.

Spec already comes with a predefined set of basic presenters (widgets) ready to use in your presenters. You can find them in the 'scripting - widgets' protocol of the `SpPresenter` class. You will find buttons, labels, checkboxes, text input, drop lists, lists, menus, tables, trees, toolbars, action bars, but also more complex widgets like code diff presenters and notebooks. You can easily instantiate a new presenter and display it:

```
SpButtonPresenter new
  label: 'ok';
  open
```

A presenter may also have a model that is a domain object you need to interact with to display or update data. In this case, your presenter class should inherit from `SpPresenterWithModel` so that the presenter keeps a reference to the domain object and updates when the model changes (see Chapter 6).

A presenter defines layouts. One is mandatory. If you want to display a presenter with the default layout, you can use the `open` or `openDialog` methods. The former will open a new window with the presenter while the latter will open a blocking dialog with the presenter. You can use `openWithLayout:` or `openDialogWithLayout:` to open the presenter with the layout you will provide as an argument.

4.4 Application

A Spec application (an instance of the `SpApplication` class hierarchy) handles your application initialization, configuration, and resources. `SpApplication` is not a presenter because it does not have a graphical representation. An instance of `SpApplication` defines your application (keeping the backend, theme, icons, and other graphical resources), and keeps the opened windows that belong to the application, but it is not shown itself.

A Spec application also provides a way to access windows or resources such as icons, and provides abstractions for interactions with the user (inform, error, file, or directory selection).

Finally, an application provides the style used by Spec to style UI elements. A default style is available, but you can customize it as shown in Chapter 15.

You should also define a method to tell what is the main window / presenter to use when running the application. Here we specialize the method `start` as follows:

```
MyApplication >> start

  (MyMainPresenter newApplication: self) open
```

You can run your application with `MyApplication new run`. It will call the `start` method you defined.

4.5 Application configuration

In the application initialization, you can configure the backend you want to use: Morphic (default) or GTK. In the future, Spec will also support Toplo, a new widget library built on top of Bloc. It will replace Morphic.

Using Morphic

Here is an example using the Film application from Chapter 3. We define a configuration as a subclass of `SpMorphicConfiguration`.

```
SpMorphicConfiguration << #ImdbMorphicConfiguration
  package: 'CodeOfSpec20Book'
```

Then we define the method `configure:` as follows:

```
ImdbMorphicConfiguration >> configure: anApplication

  super configure: anApplication.
  "There are ways to write/read this from strings or files,
   but this is how you do it programatically."
  self styleSheet
    addClass: 'header' with: [ :style |
      style
        addPropertyFontWith: [ :font | font bold: true ];
        addPropertyDrawWith: [ :draw | draw color: Color red ] ]
```

Note that we could use a style described in a string as shown Chapter 15.

Finally, in the corresponding application class, we declare that the Morphic backend should use our configuration using the message `useBackend:with:`.

```
ImdbApp >> initialize

  super initialize.
  self useBackend: #Morphic with: ImdbMorphicConfiguration new
```

Using GTK theme and settings

For GTK the process is similar, we define a subclass of `SpGTKConfiguration`.

```
SpGTKConfiguration << #ImdbGTKConfiguration
  package: 'CodeOfSpec20Book'
```

Then we configure it by selecting and extending CSS.

```
ImdbGTKConfiguration >> configure: anApplication

  super configure: anApplication.
  "This will choose the theme 'Sierra-dark' if it is available"
  self installTheme: 'Sierra-dark'.
  "This will add a 'provider' (a stylesheet)"
  self addCSSProviderFromString: '.header {color: red; font-weight:
    bold}'
```

And in the application initialization, we declare that the configuration should be used for GTK.

```
ImdbApp >> initialize

  super initialize.
  self useBackend: #GTK with: ImdbGTKConfiguration new
```

4.6 Layouts

To display its elements, a presenter uses a layout. A layout describes how elements are placed on the display surface. To help you build nice user interfaces, several layouts are available:

- **GridLayout:** Choose this layout when you need to create a presenter with a label, and fields that need to be aligned (form style). You can specify in which box of the grid you want to place an element.

- **BoxLayout:** a `SpBoxLayout` arranges presenters in a box, vertically (top to bottom) or horizontally (left to right).

- **PanedLayout:** a `SpPanedLayout` is a layout with two elements called "panes" and a splitter in between. The user can drag the splitter to resize the panes.

- **TabLayout:** a `SpTabLayout` shows all its elements as tabs. You can select a tab to display the content.

- **MillerLayout:** a layout to implement miller columns, also known as cascading lists (https://en.wikipedia.org/wiki/Miller_columns).

Spec core in a nutshell

Any layout in Spec is dynamic and composable. In general, a layout is defined at the presenter instance level, but it can be defined on the class side.

Defining a layout is as simple as defining the defaultLayout method. This method is automatically invoked if a layout is not manually set.

Let's revisit the defaultLayout method from Chapter 2.

```
CustomerSatisfactionPresenter >> defaultLayout

    ^ SpBoxLayout newTopToBottom
        add: (SpBoxLayout newLeftToRight
            add: buttonHappy;
            add: buttonNeutral;
            add: buttonBad;
            yourself);
        add: result;
        yourself
```

The method defines two box layouts:

- one containing the three buttons
- one containing the first one and a result text below.

Each of the layouts refers to accessible subpresenters (buttonHappy, buttonNeutral, buttonBad, result) from the presenter. Figure 4-3 shows the corresponding result.

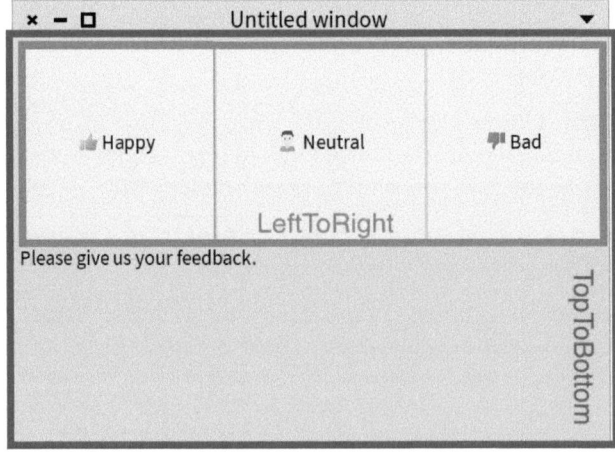

Figure 4-3 The layout corresponding to the defaultLayout method.

44

4.7 Styles and stylesheets

A Spec application always comes with a default stylesheet. A stylesheet contains style definitions that can be applied to presenters. Chapter 15 presents styles in detail.

A style is a property container to "style" components, and defines (to a certain degree) its behavior within the different layouts.

Here is an example of a stylesheet for the Morphic backend:

```
'.application [
  .lightGreen [ Draw { #color: #B3E6B5 } ],
  .lightBlue [ Draw { #color: #lightBlue } ] ]'
```

The styles in Spec format are similar to CSS but expressed in STON. Pay attention not to forget the leading periods.

You can apply it on your Spec application by sending the `styleSheet:` message to an application:

```
myStyleSheet := SpStyleVariableSTONReader fromString:
  '.application [
     Font { #bold: true },
     .bgBlack [ Draw { #backgroundColor: #black } ],
     .blue [ Draw { #color: #blue } ]
  ]'
application styleSheet: SpStyle defaultStyleSheet, myStyleSheet.
```

Then you can style a presenter using the message `addStyle:` (think about a tag with a class in CSS) as follows:

```
presenter label: 'I am a label'.
presenter addStyle: 'blue'.
```

4.8 Navigation between presenters

Once the definition of your UI components (i.e., your Spec presenters and layouts) is done, you will need to define the behavior of the UI: what happens when you open a new presenter?

You will probably want to provide some data (a model) to the presenter so that it can be used to display data. It is called a transmission: you transmit data from one presenter to another presenter. Transmissions are defined as reactions to events.

It is quite easy to define the behavior of the UI by using widget-predefined events. You can find them in the api-events protocol of the presenter classes.

Most used events are whenSelectionChangedDo:, whenModelChangedDo:, whenTextChangedDo:. Here are some examples:

```
messageList
   whenSelectionChangedDo: [ :selection |
      messageDetail model: selection selectedItem ];
   whenModelChangedDo: [ self updateTitle ].
textModel whenSubmitDo: [ :text | self accept: text ].
addButton action: [ self addDirectory ].
filterInput whenTextChangedDo: [ :text | self refreshTable ].
```

4.9 Conclusion

Class SpPresenter is a central class that has the following responsibilities:

- Initialization of presenter part and state.
- Definition of application layout.
- Connection of the elements to support the interaction flow.
- Update of the UI components.

We will illustrate these points in the following chapters.

CHAPTER 5

Testing Spec applications

Developers often think that testing a user interface is difficult. It is true that fully testing the placement and layout of widgets can be tedious. However, testing the logic of an application and in particular the interaction logic is possible. That is what we will show in this chapter. We will show that testing a Spec application is simple and effective.

5.1 Testing presenters

Tests are key to ensuring that everything works correctly. In addition, they free us from the fear of breaking something without being warned about it. Tests support refactorings. While such facts are general and applicable to many domains, they are also true for user interfaces.

Spec architecture

Spec is based on an architecture with three different layers as shown in Figure 5-1:

- **Presenters:** Presenters define the interaction logic and manipulate domain objects. They access backend widgets but via an API that is specified by Adapters.
- **Adapters:** Adapters are objects exposing low-level backend widgets. They are a bridge between presenters and low-level widgets.
- **Backend widgets**. Backend widgets are plain widgets that can be used without Spec.

Testing Spec applications

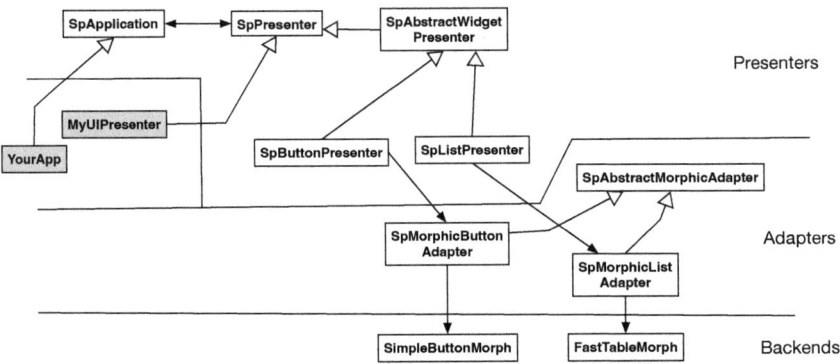

Figure 5-1 Spec Architecture: three layers Presenters - Adapters - Backends.

Three roles and concerns

To help you understand the different possibilities of testing that you can engage in, we identify the following roles and their related concerns.

- **Spec Users.** Spec users are developers who build a new application. They define the logic of the application by assembling presenters and domain objects. We believe that this is the role that you will play most of the time.

- **Spec Developers.** Spec developers are more concerned with the development of new Spec presenters and their link with the adapters.

- **Widget Developers.** Widget developers are concerned about the logic and working of a given widget for a given backend.

Spec user perspective

We will focus on the first role. For the reader interested in the second role, the class `SpAbstractBackendForTest` is a good starting place.

As a Spec user, you should consider that the backends are working and your responsibility is to test the logic of the user interface components. You should make sure that when the model changes, the user interface components reflect the changes. Inversely when the user interface components change, you should ensure that the model is updated. Let's give an example.

5.2 Spec user example

We will test a simple spec application, as shown in Figure 5-2. The model for this application is an instance of the Color class. The application shows a list of colors from which the user can choose one. After choosing a color, the application shows the color in a big box, and it shows the printString of the color, together with the hexadecimal code. The application also provides two buttons to make the chosen color lighter or darker.

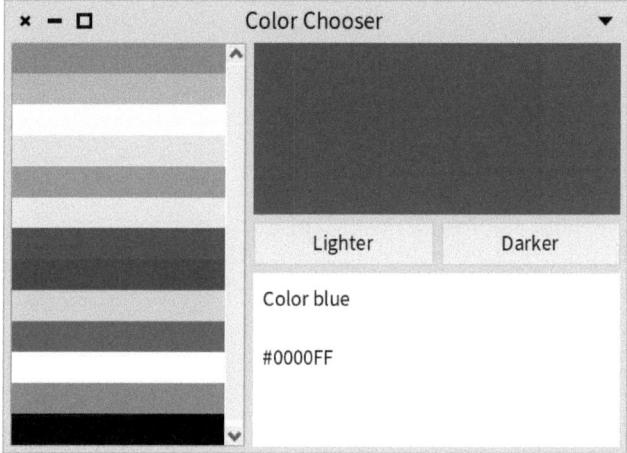

Figure 5-2 A Spec application.

The presenter is defined as described below. The class has six instance variables. The first five instance variables hold subpresenters that compose the application window. The sixth instance variable holds the color that serves as the model of the application.

```
SpPresenter << #ColorChooser
    slots: { #colorList . #colorDetails . #colorBox . #lighterButton .
      #darkerButton . #currentColor };
    package: 'CodeOfSpec20Book'
```

The method initializePresenters initializes the subpresenters. colorList holds a list presenter with the colors. colorBox displays the chosen color in a SpRoassalPresenter. colorDetails holds a text presenter that shows information about the color. lighterButton and darkerButton are the buttons to make the current color lighter or darker.

```
ColorChooser >> initializePresenters

  colorList := self newList
    display: [ :color | '' ];
    displayBackgroundColor: [ :color | color ];
    yourself.
  colorBox := self instantiate: SpRoassalPresenter.
  lighterButton := self newButton
    label: 'Lighter';
    action: [ self lighter ];
    yourself.
  darkerButton := self newButton
    label: 'Darker';
    action: [ self darker ];
    yourself.
  colorDetails := self newText
```

The instance variable currentColor is not initialized by initializePresenters. It is initialized in setModelBeforeInitialization: because a color can be given when creating a new ColorChooser instance.

```
ColorChooser >> setModelBeforeInitialization: aColor

  currentColor := aColor
```

The method defaultLayout defines the layout with a left side and a right side. The left side is the color list. The right side consists of the color box, the two buttons, and the color details. Composition with horizontal and vertical BoxLayouts, together with a 5-pixel spacing, results in the window shown in Figure 5-2.

```
ColorChooser >> defaultLayout

  | colorBoxAndDetails buttons |
  buttons := SpBoxLayout newLeftToRight
    spacing: 5;
    add: lighterButton;
    add: darkerButton;
    yourself.
  colorBoxAndDetails := SpBoxLayout newTopToBottom
    spacing: 5;
    add: colorBox;
    add: buttons expand: false;
    add: colorDetails;
    yourself.
  ^ SpBoxLayout newLeftToRight
    spacing: 5;
    add: colorList expand: false;
```

5.2 Spec user example

```
    add: colorBoxAndDetails;
    yourself
```

The method `initializeWindow:` sets the title and the initial dimensions of the window.

```
ColorChooser >> initializeWindow: aWindowPresenter

  aWindowPresenter
    title: 'Color Chooser';
    initialExtent: 400@294
```

Connecting the subpresenters is expressed easily. When a selection in the color list is made, the color is updated.

```
ColorChooser >> connectPresenters

  colorList whenSelectionChangedDo: [ :selection |
    self updateColor: selection selectedItem ]
```

The method `connectPresenters` delegates to `updateColor:` to update the color box and the color details. As you can see, `updateColor:` takes care of a possible `nil` value for `currentColor`.

```
ColorChooser >> updateColor: color

  | details |
  currentColor := color.
  colorBox canvas
    background: (currentColor ifNil: [ Color transparent ]);
    signalUpdate.
  details := currentColor
    ifNil: [ '' ]
    ifNotNil: [ self detailsFor: currentColor ].
  colorDetails text: details
```

The method `updateColor:` delegates the responsibility of producing the text with color details to `detailsFor:`.

```
ColorChooser >> detailsFor: color

  ^ String streamContents: [ :stream |
    stream
      print: color; cr; cr; nextPut: $#;
      nextPutAll: color asHexString ]
```

We also define `updatePresenter` to set the initial state of the subpresenters. It populates the color list with default colors, as defined by `defaultColors`, and the initial color is set with `updateColor:`.

```
ColorChooser >> updatePresenter

    | initialColor |
    initialColor := currentColor.
    colorList items: self defaultColors.
    self updateColor: initialColor
```

Note that keeping the initial color with `initialColor := currentColor` is necessary because `colorList items: self defaultColors` resets the selection in the list, which triggers the block in `connectPresenters`. That block sends `updateColor: nil` because there is no selection. So this method keeps the initial color and applies it with `self updateColor: initialColor`.

To keep things simple, `defaultColors` answers only a handful of colors. This method can be changed easily to answer a different collection of colors. For instance, you could try `Color red wheel: 20`.

```
ColorChooser >> defaultColors

    ^ {
    Color red .
    Color orange .
    Color yellow .
    Color green .
    Color magenta .
    Color cyan .
    Color blue .
    Color purple .
    Color pink .
    Color brown .
    Color white .
    Color gray .
    Color black }
```

There are only two methods missing from the code above to complete the class implementation. The method `initializePresenters` sets actions for the buttons, which invoke the following two methods. These methods delegate to the method `updateColor:` to do the heavy lifting.

```
ColorChooser >> lighter

    self updateColor: currentColor lighter
```

```
ColorChooser >> darker

    self updateColor: currentColor darker
```

With the code above in place, we can open the application. Let's start with opening the default with:

```
[ColorChooser new open
```

In this case, there is no initial color, which results in the window shown in Figure 5-3. The color box does not show a color and the color details are empty.

Figure 5-3 The default ColorChooser.

Let's see what happens when we provide a color with:

```
[(ColorChooser on: Color yellow) open
```

In this case, yellow is given as the initial color that should be shown when the window opens. Note that on: has not been defined as a class method by ColorChooser. The class method is inherited from the superclass SpAbstractPresenter. The result is shown in Figure 5-4.

5.3 Tests

With all the code in place, it is time to write some tests. First, we define the test class.

```
TestCase << #ColorChooserTest
    slots: { #chooser };
    package: 'CodeOfSpec20Book'
```

Each test will open a new instance of ColorChooser. It is expected that the instance variable chooser will hold the instance used in a test. To ensure that the instance is cleaned up, we define tearDown. It takes into account that a test can fail before chooser is bound to an instance of ColorChooser.

Figure 5-4 The ColorChooser opened on the color yellow.

```
ColorChooserTest >> tearDown

  chooser ifNotNil: [ chooser delete ].
  super tearDown
```

With that infrastructure in place, we can write our tests.

Opening the default application

Our first test describes the state of the application after opening the default application.

```
ColorChooserTest >> testDefault
  "When a ColorChooser opens without a color,
   the color box shows a transparent color and the details are empty."

  chooser := ColorChooser new.
  chooser open.

  self assert: chooser boxColor equals: Color transparent.
  self assert: chooser detailsText equals: ''
```

We have to add a few so-called 'test support' methods to make this work. These methods belong to the test api of the ColorChooser, because they are intended to be used for testing purposes only.

54

5.3 Tests

```
ColorChooser >> boxColor

  ^ colorBox canvas color
```

```
ColorChooser >> detailsText

  ^ colorDetails text
```

Correct initialization

The second test describes the state of the application after opening the application with a color.

```
ColorChooserTest >> testInitialization
  "When a ColorChooser opens on a color,
   the color box shows that color
   and the details show the print string and the HEX code."

  chooser := ColorChooser on: Color palePeach.
  chooser open.

  self assert: chooser boxColor equals: Color palePeach.
  self assert: chooser detailsText equals: 'Color palePeach\\#FFEDD5'
    withCRs
```

Choosing a color

The third test describes what happens when the user chooses a color.

First, the test selects the first color in the list and verifies the state of the subpresenters. Then it selects the seventh color in the list and verifies the expected state changes in the subpresenters.

```
ColorChooserTest >> testChooseColor
  "When the user chooses a color in the list,
   the color box shows the color
   and the details show the print string and the HEX code."

  chooser := ColorChooser new.
  chooser open.

  chooser clickColorAtIndex: 1.
  self assert: chooser boxColor equals: Color red.
  self assert: chooser detailsText equals: 'Color red\\#FF0000'
    withCRs.

  chooser clickColorAtIndex: 7.
  self assert: chooser boxColor equals: Color blue.
```

55

```
self assert: chooser detailsText equals: 'Color blue\\#0000FF'
    withCRs
```

This test uses an extra test support method to click on a color in the list.

```
ColorChooser >> clickColorAtIndex: index

    colorList clickAtIndex: index
```

Making the current color lighter

Now, it is time to describe the application behavior after clicking the 'Lighter' button.

The test consists of four parts. First, the first color in the list is clicked. That results in an update of the color box and the color details. After a click on the button, the test verifies the changed state of the color box and the color details. Then it clicks the button a second time to describe that the current color can be made lighter over and over again. Finally, the test selects the seventh color in the list and verifies the expected state changes in the subpresenters.

```
ColorChooserTest >> testLighter
   "When the user presses the 'Lighter' button,
    the color box shows the ligher color
    and the details show the print string and the HEX code."

   chooser := ColorChooser new.
   chooser open.

   chooser clickColorAtIndex: 1.
   chooser clickLighterButton.
   self
      assert: chooser boxColor
      equals: (Color r: 1.0 g: 0.030303030303030304 b:
      0.030303030303030304 alpha: 1.0).
   self
      assert: chooser detailsText
      equals: '(Color r: 1.0 g: 0.030303030303030304 b:
      0.030303030303030304 alpha: 1.0)\\#FF0707' withCRs.

   chooser clickLighterButton.
   self
      assert: chooser boxColor
      equals: (Color r: 1.0 g: 0.06060606060606061 b:
      0.06060606060606061 alpha: 1.0).
   self
      assert: chooser detailsText
      equals: '(Color r: 1.0 g: 0.06060606060606061 b:
```

5.3 Tests

```
    0.06060606060606061 alpha: 1.0)\\#FF0F0F' withCRs.

  chooser clickColorAtIndex: 7.
  chooser clickLighterButton.
  self
    assert: chooser boxColor
    equals: (Color r: 0.030303030303030304 g: 0.030303030303030304 b:
    1.0 alpha: 1.0).
  self
    assert: chooser detailsText
    equals: '(Color r: 0.030303030303030304 g: 0.030303030303030304 b:
    1.0 alpha: 1.0)\\#0707FF' withCRs
```

As the other tests, this test requires an extra test support method.

```
ColorChooser >> clickLighterButton

  lighterButton click
```

Making the current color darker

This test is very similar to the previous test. Instead of clicking the 'Lighter' button, this test clicks the 'Darker' button.

```
ColorChooserTest >> testDarker
  "When the user presses the 'Darker' button,
   the color box shows the darker color
   and the details show the print string and the HEX code."

  chooser := ColorChooser new.
  chooser open.

  chooser clickColorAtIndex: 1.
  chooser clickDarkerButton.
  self
    assert: chooser boxColor
    equals: (Color r: 0.9198435972629521 g: 0.0 b: 0.0 alpha: 1.0).
  self
    assert: chooser detailsText
    equals: '(Color r: 0.9198435972629521 g: 0.0 b: 0.0 alpha:
    1.0)\\#EB0000' withCRs.

  chooser clickDarkerButton.
  self
    assert: chooser boxColor
    equals: (Color r: 0.8396871945259042 g: 0.0 b: 0.0 alpha: 1.0).
  self
    assert: chooser detailsText
```

```
    equals: '(Color r: 0.8396871945259042 g: 0.0 b: 0.0 alpha:
    1.0)\\#D60000' withCRs.

chooser clickColorAtIndex: 7.
chooser clickDarkerButton.
self
    assert: chooser boxColor
    equals: (Color r: 0.0 g: 0.0 b: 0.9198435972629521 alpha: 1.0).
self
    assert: chooser detailsText
    equals: '(Color r: 0.0 g: 0.0 b: 0.9198435972629521 alpha:
    1.0)\\#0000EB' withCRs
```

Again, this test requires an extra test support method. Note that such a method is not mandatory and could be replaced by a simple access to the button using an accessor. Using such a helper method factors the logic.

```
ColorChooser >> clickDarkerButton

    darkerButton click
```

Verifying window properties

Now we want to check that the window is built correctly. We will verify that the title and the initial extent of the window are correct.

```
ColorChooserTest >> testInitializeWindow

    | window |
    chooser := ColorChooser new.
    window := chooser open.
    self assert: window isBuilt.
    self assert: window title equals: 'Color Chooser'.
    self assert: window initialExtent equals: 400@294
```

5.4 Testing your application

In Spec, an application is responsible to run and gather the windows of your application. The pattern is to override the `start` method of your application. The method `start` is a hook method that is invoked when you execute your application using the `run` message as in `ColorChooserApplication new run`.

It is important to see that in the `start` method you should configure the presenter you are opening so that it knows its application. This is important so that the application knows the windows it is opening.

In a TDD fashion, we define the test class first:

5.5 Known limitations and conclusion

```
TestCase << #ColorChooserApplicationTest
    slots: { #application };
    package: 'CodeOfSpec20Book'
```

```
ColorChooserApplicationTest >> setUp

    super setUp.
    application := ColorChooserApplication new
```

```
ColorChooserApplicationTest >> tearDown

    application ifNotNil: [ application closeAllWindows ].
    super tearDown
```

```
ColorChooserApplicationTest >> testWindowRegistration

    self assert: application windows size equals: 0.
    application start.
    self assert: application windows size equals: 1.
    application start.
    self assert: application windows size equals: 2
```

The method `testWindowRegistration` describes the expected behavior of our application. When opened windows are correctly registered, the application should have access to all the opened windows. The test opens two windows and verifies that the number of windows increases.

The test fails, because `ColorChooserApplication` does not exist yet. Let's define it:

```
SpApplication << #ColorChooserApplication
    slots: {};
    package: 'CodeOfSpec20Book'
```

The test still fails. It fails in the second assertion because the application does not register the open windows. Let's implement the `start` method to register the windows.

```
ColorChooserApplication >> start

    ColorChooser new
        application: self;
        open
```

Tada! The test passes.

5.5 Known limitations and conclusion

In this chapter we showed that you can take advantage of Spec to define tests that will help you to evolve the visual part of your application. This is really key for modern software development and to lower your stress in the future. So take advantage of agile development.

Currently, Spec does not offer a way to script and control popup windows. It is not possible to script a button that opens a dialog for a value. Future versions of Spec should cover this missing feature.

CHAPTER 6

The dual aspects of presenters: Domain and interaction model

A presenter has a dual role in Spec. On the one hand, it acts as the glue between domain objects and widgets, and on the other hand, it implements the user interface logic by connecting subpresenters together. These two aspects compose the core of a presenter and this is what this chapter describes.

We start by presenting an important aspect of presenters: the way they handle communication with domain objects that here we call a model.

In this chapter, we visit the key aspects of Spec and put the important customization points of its building process in perspective.

6.1 About presenters on a model

Frequently you want to open a presenter on a given object such as your list of to-do items. In that case, you would like the subpresenters (list, text,..) to be initialized based on the object that you passed. For example, you may want to get all the items in your basket.

However, simply instantiating a presenter using the message new and passing the object will not work because messages such as `initializePresenters` will be already sent.

There are two ways to address this situation in Spec and in particular, Spec offers a special presenter called `SpPresenterWithModel`. Let us explain how to take advantage of it.

We will build the simplest example to show how to do it. We will implement a presenter that lists the method signatures of a class, first using a presenter inheriting from the default superclass (SpPresenter) and second using a presenter (subclass of SpPresenterWithModel) dedicated to handling a model.

6.2 Example with SpPresenter

If you do not need to react to model changes, you can simply inherit from SpPresenter, override the setModelBeforeInitialization: method to set your domain object, and use YourPresenter on: yourDomainObject to instantiate it.

This is exactly what we do hereafter.

First, we create a new presenter class.

```
SpPresenter << #MethodLister
    slots: { #sourceClass . #list};
    package: 'Spec2Book'
```

We define a list presenter and populate it.

```
MethodLister >> initializePresenters

    list := self newList.
    list items: sourceClass selectors sorted
```

Specializing the method setModelBeforeInitialization:, we assign its argument coming from the on: message to the instance variable sourceClass for future use.

```
MethodLister >> setModelBeforeInitialization: aModel

    sourceClass := aModel
```

We define a basic layout for the list presenter.

```
MethodLister >> defaultLayout

    ^ SpBoxLayout newTopToBottom
        add: #list;
        yourself
```

The following snippet opens a window with the list of methods of the class Point as shown in Figure 6-1.

```
(MethodLister on: Point) open.
```

Figure 6-1 A simple list of sorted selectors of the class Point.

6.3 SpPresenter vs. SpPresenterWithModel

The key difference between using `SpPresenter` and `SpPresenterWithModel` is if you need to react to changes of the model. We mean that while the presenter is open, an event changes the model that was used to build the UI. In our example, that means that when you change the class, the method list displays its selectors. If you need this behavior, then you should use `SpPresenterWithModel`.

The following snippet shows that the change of model is not taken into account in the sense that the list is not refreshed and still displays methods of the class `Point`, while the methods of the class 'Rectangle should be displayed.

```
| lister |
lister := MethodLister on: Point.
lister open.
lister setModel: Rectangle
```

6.4 Example with SpPresenterWithModel

A presenter may also have a model that is a domain object you need to interact with to display or update data. In that case, you should inherit from `SpPresenterWithModel` so that the presenter keeps a reference to the domain object and manages its changes. As a client of this presenter, we use the message `model:` to change the model.

The method is inherited from the superclass. This `model:` method implements the following behavior:

- If the domain object is an instance of `Model`, it is stored as is in the presenter.

- Else a value holder is created to hold the domain object so that you can be notified when the domain object used by the presenter changes.

You do not need to define the method `setModelBeforeInitialization:` as we previously showed.

Let us revisit our little example. First, we inherit from `SpPresenterWithModel`.

```
SpPresenterWithModel << #MethodListerWithModel
    slots: { #list };
    package: 'Spec2Book'
```

Second, we define `initializePresenters`.

```
MethodListerWithModel >> initializePresenters

    list := self newList
```

You can then implement the `modelChanged` method to refresh your UI when the model changes.

```
MethodListerWithModel >> modelChanged

    list items: self model selectors sorted
```

We define the same layout method as before:

```
MethodListerWithModel >> defaultLayout

    ^ SpBoxLayout newTopToBottom
        add: #list;
        yourself
```

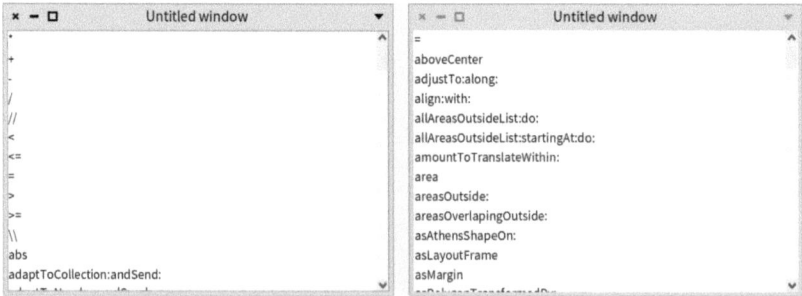

Figure 6-2 A simple list of sorted selectors changing based on its model.

Now we can open our widget. As the following script shows, it will react to the change of the model (see Figure 6-2).

6.5 User interface building: a model of UI presentation

```
| lister |
lister := MethodListerWithModel on: Point.
lister open.
lister model: Rectangle
```

Note that the right way to create a presenter is to use the method `newApplication: anApplication` because it ensures that the application knows its constituents.

So the code above should be:

```
| lister app |
app := SpApplication new
lister := MethodListerWithModel newApplication: app.
```

Then we have a problem because we want to specify the model too. The correct and idiomatic way is to use the method `newApplication:model:` so the final code version is:

```
| lister |
app := SpApplication new.
lister := MethodListerWithModel newApplication: app model: Point.
lister open.
lister model: Rectangle
```

You saw that you can easily build an application user interface populated from a model and reacting to model changes.

Now we will focus on the user interface logic modeling.

6.5 User interface building: a model of UI presentation

A key aspect of Spec is that all user interfaces are constructed through the reuse and composition of existing user interfaces. To allow this, defining a user interface consists of defining the *model* of the user interface, and *not* the user interface elements that will be shown on screen. These UI elements are instantiated by Spec, taking into account the underlying UI framework.

In the end, it is the presentation model and the UI elements that make up the resulting user interface that is shown. This composition of the presentation models is represented as a Presenter object as in Model-View-Presenter. The presenter that is defined in Spec corresponds to a presenter in the MVP triad as shown in Figure 6-3.

To define a new user interface, the developer should create a subclass of SpPresenter.

Fundamentally, it is built around three concerns that materialize themselves as the following three methods in SpPresenter:

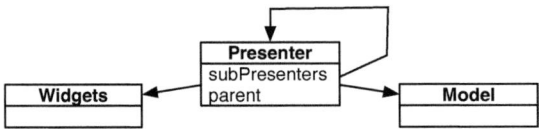

Figure 6-3 A presenter is a model of presentation: It is in relationships with the widgets and its domain model. It composes other presenters to form a presenter tree.

- The method initializePresenters treats the subpresenters themselves.
- The method connectPresenters treats the interactions between the subpresenters.
- The method defaultLayout treats the layout of the subpresenters.

Hence, these methods are typically found in the model of each user interface. You can read the code of the small interface presented in Chapter 2 to get examples of each of the points we will present now.

In this chapter, we describe the finer points of each method and how these three methods work together to build the overall UI.

6.6 The *initializePresenters* method

The method initializePresenters instantiates, holds in instance variables, and partially configures the different widgets that will be part of the UI.

The instantiation of the presentation models will cause the instantiation and initialization of the different lower-level user interface components, constructing the UI that is shown to the user. The first part of the configuration of each widget is specified in initializePresenters as well.

The focus of this method is to specify what the widgets will look like and what their self-contained behavior is. The behavior to update the model state, e.g., when pressing a Save button, is described in this method as well. It is explicitly *not* the responsibility of this method to define the interactions *between* the widgets.

In general, the initializePresenters method should follow the pattern:

- Widget instantiation
- Widget configuration
- Specification of focus order

The last step is not mandatory since the focus order is by default given by the order of declaration of the subpresenters.

Note. Specifying the method `initializePresenters` is mandatory, as without it the UI would have no widgets.

Subpresenter instantiation

The instantiation of a subpresenter (i.e., the model for a widget composing the UI) can be done in two ways: through the use of a creation method or through the use of the `instantiate:` method.

- Considering the first option, the framework provides unary messages for the creation of all basic widgets. The format of these messages is `new[Widget]`, for example, `newButton` creates a button widget, and `newList` creates a list widget. The complete list of available widget creation methods can be found in the class `SpPresenter` in the protocol `scripting - widgets`.

- The second option is more general: to reuse a `SpPresenter` subclass (other than the ones handled by the first option), the widget needs to be instantiated using the `instantiate:` method. For example, to reuse a `MessageBrowser` presenter, the code is `self instantiate: MessageBrowser`. The `instantiate:` method has the responsibility to build an internal parent presenter tree.

6.7 The *connectPresenters* method

The method `connectPresenters` defines the interactions between the different widgets. By connecting the behaviors of the different widgets, it specifies the overall presentation, i.e., how the overall UI responds to interactions by the user. Usually, this method consists of specifications of actions to perform when a certain event is received by a widget. The whole interaction flow of the UI then emerges from the propagation of those events.

Note. The method `connectPresenters` is an optional method for a Spec UI, but we recommend to separate this behavior clearly.

In Spec, the different UI models are contained in value holders, and the event mechanism relies on the announcements from these value holders to manage the interactions between widgets.

Value holders provide the method `whenChangedDo:` that is used to register a block to perform on change, and the method `whenChangedSend: aSelector to: aReceiver` to send a message to a given object. In addition to these primitive methods, the basic widgets provide more specific hooks, e.g., when an item in a list is selected (`whenSelectionChangedDo:`).

6.8 The *defaultLayout* method

Widget layout is defined by specifying methods that state how the different widgets are placed in the UI. In addition, it also specifies how a widget reacts when the window is resized. As we will see later, these methods can have different names.

The method `defaultLayout` is an instance method, but it can be also defined at the class level. Put differently, typically all the instances of the same user interface have the same layout, but a layout can be specific to one instance and be dynamic.

Note. Specifying a layout is mandatory, as without it the UI would show no widgets to the user.

Using setter message `layout:`

We recommend to clearly separate presenter initialization (`initializePresenters` and `defaultLayout`). You can, however, also use the `layout:` message to set a layout during the presenter initialization phase.

Multiple layouts for a widget

For the same UI, multiple layouts can be described, and when the UI is built, the use of a specific layout can be indicated. To do this, instead of calling `open` (as we have done until now), use the `openWithLayout:` message with a layout as an argument.

6.9 Conclusion

In this chapter, we have given a more detailed description of how the three fundamental methods of Spec, `initializePresenters`, `defaultLayout`, and `connectPresenters`, are each responsible for a different aspect of the user interface building process.

Although reuse is fundamental in Spec, we did not explicitly treat it in this chapter. Instead, we refer to the next chapter for more information.

CHAPTER 7

Reuse and composition at work

A key design goal of Spec is to enable the seamless reuse of user interfaces. The reason for this is that it results in a significant productivity boost when creating user interfaces.

This focus on reuse was actually already visible in the previous chapters, where we have seen that basic widgets can be used as if they were complete user interfaces. In this section we focus on the reuse and composition of presenters, showing that it basically comes for free. The only requirement when building a UI is to consider how the user interface should be parameterized when it is being reused.

Said differently, in this chapter, you will learn how you can build a new UI by reusing already defined elements.

7.1 First requirements

To show how Spec enables the composition and reuse of user interfaces, in this chapter we build the user interface shown in Figure 7-1 as a composition of four parts:

1. The **WidgetClassListPresenter**: This widget contains a `SpListPresenter` specifically for displaying the subclasses of `SpAbstractWidgetPresenter`.

2. The **ProtocolMethodListPresenter**: This widget is composed of a `SpListPresenter` and a `SpLabelPresenter` for displaying methods of a protocol.

Reuse and composition at work

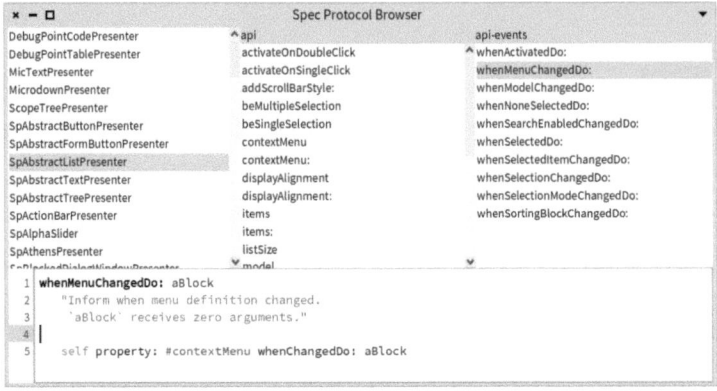

Figure 7-1 ProtocolCodeBrowser: Browsing the public APIs of widgets.

3. The **ProtocolViewerPresenter**: This widget is a composition of one `WidgetClassListPresenter` and two `ProtocolMethodListPresenter`. It allows browsing the methods of all subclasses of `SpAbstractWidgetPresenter`.

4. The **ProtocolCodeBrowserPresenter**: This widget reuses a `ProtocolViewerPresenter`, changes its layout, and adds a `SpTextPresenter` to see the source code of the methods.

7.2 Creating a basic UI to be reused as a widget

The first UI we build displays a list of all subclasses of the class `SpAbstractWidgetPresenter`. This UI will later be reused as a widget for a more complete UI. The code is as follows.

First, we create a subclass of `SpPresenter` with one instance variable `list` which will hold an instance of `SpListPresenter`.

```
SpPresenter << #WidgetClassListPresenter
    slots: { #list };
    package: 'CodeOfSpec20Book'
```

In the method `initializePresenters`, we create the list and populate it with the required classes, in alphabetical order.

```
WidgetClassListPresenter >> initializePresenters

    list := self newList.
    list items: (SpAbstractWidgetPresenter allSubclasses sorted: [:a :b
```

7.3 Supporting reuse

```
    | a name < b name ]).
  self focusOrder add: list
```

We also add a title for the window.

```
WidgetClassListPresenter >> initializeWindow: aWindowPresenter

  aWindowPresenter title: 'Widgets'
```

The layout contains only the list.

```
WidgetClassListPresenter >> defaultLayout

  ^ SpBoxLayout newLeftToRight
      add: #list;
      yourself
```

When doing `WidgetClassListPresenter new open`, you should see the UI shown in Figure 7-2.

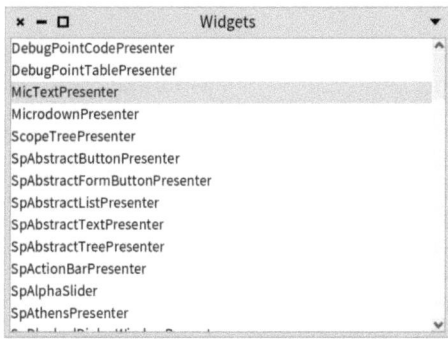

Figure 7-2 WidgetClassListPresenter.

7.3 Supporting reuse

Since this UI will later be used together with other widgets to provide a more complete user interface, some actions will need to occur when a list item is clicked. However, we cannot know beforehand what all these possible actions will be everywhere that it will be reused. Therefore the best solution is to place this responsibility on the reuser of the widget. Every time this UI is reused as a widget, it will be configured by the reuser. To allow this, we add a configuration method named `whenSelectionChangedDo:` as follows:

```
WidgetClassListPresenter >> whenSelectionChangedDo: aBlock

    list whenSelectionChangedDo: aBlock
```

Now, whoever reuses this widget can parameterize it with a block that will be executed whenever the selection changes.

7.4 Combining two basic presenters into a reusable UI

The UI we build next will show a list of all methods of a given protocol, and it combines two widgets: a list and a label. Considering reuse, there is no difference from the previous UI. This is because the reuse of a UI as a widget is *not impacted at all* by the number of widgets it contains (nor by their position). Large and complex UIs are reused in the same way as simple widgets.

```
SpPresenter << #ProtocolMethodListPresenter
    slots: { #label . #methods };
    package: 'CodeOfSpec20Book'
```

The `initializePresenters` method for this UI is straightforward. We specify the default label text as 'Protocol', which will be changed when the widget is reused.

```
ProtocolMethodListPresenter >> initializePresenters

    methods := self newList.
    methods display: [ :m | m selector ].
    label := self newLabel.
    label label: 'Protocol'.
    self focusOrder add: methods
```

To make sure that we have a nice title when the widget is opened in a window, we define the method `initializeWindow:`.

```
ProtocolMethodListPresenter >> initializeWindow: aWindowPresenter

    aWindowPresenter title: 'Protocol widget'
```

The layout code builds a column with the label above the method list.

```
ProtocolMethodListPresenter >> defaultLayout

    ^ SpBoxLayout newTopToBottom
        add: #label;
        add: #methods;
        yourself
```

7.4 Combining two basic presenters into a reusable UI

This UI can be seen by executing `ProtocolMethodList new open`. As shown in Figure 7-3 the list is empty and the result is not really nice. This is normal because we did not set any items. We should also place the elements better.

Figure 7-3 ProtocolMethodListPresenter with bad layout.

```
ProtocolMethodListPresenter >> defaultLayout

    ^ SpBoxLayout newTopToBottom
        add: #label expand: false;
        add: #methods;
        yourself
```

Now you should get a better UI as shown in Figure 7-4.

Figure 7-4 ProtocolMethodListPresenter with nicer layout.

Our protocol method list needs to be configured when it is used, by filling the list of methods and specifying what the name of the protocol is. To allow this, we add some configuration methods:

```
ProtocolMethodListPresenter >> items: aCollection

    methods items: aCollection
```

```
ProtocolMethodListPresenter >> label: aText

    label label: aText
```

```
ProtocolMethodListPresenter >> resetSelection

    methods selection unselectAll
```

```
ProtocolMethodListPresenter >> whenSelectionChangedDo: aBlock

    methods whenSelectionChangedDo: aBlock
```

7.5 Live inspection of the widgets

Now we can check manually if the widget is working by doing:

```
ProtocolMethodListPresenter new open; inspect
```

Then in the inspector, we can use the newly created presenter to pass a collection of methods. See the result in Figure 7-5.

```
self items: Point methods
```

Now we can play and for example, decide to sort the items as follows:

```
self items: (Point methods sort: #selector ascending)
```

7.6 Writing tests

When we start to feel the need to check manually what we have done, that is a sign that we should write a test instead. It is easy to write simple tests for widgets when we do not use popups. So let's take advantage of that.

We add an accessor to access the method list.

```
ProtocolMethodListPresenter >> methods

    ^ methods
```

```
TestCase << #ProtocolMethodListPresenterTest
    slots: {};
    package: 'CodeOfSpec20Book'
```

7.7 Managing three widgets and their interactions

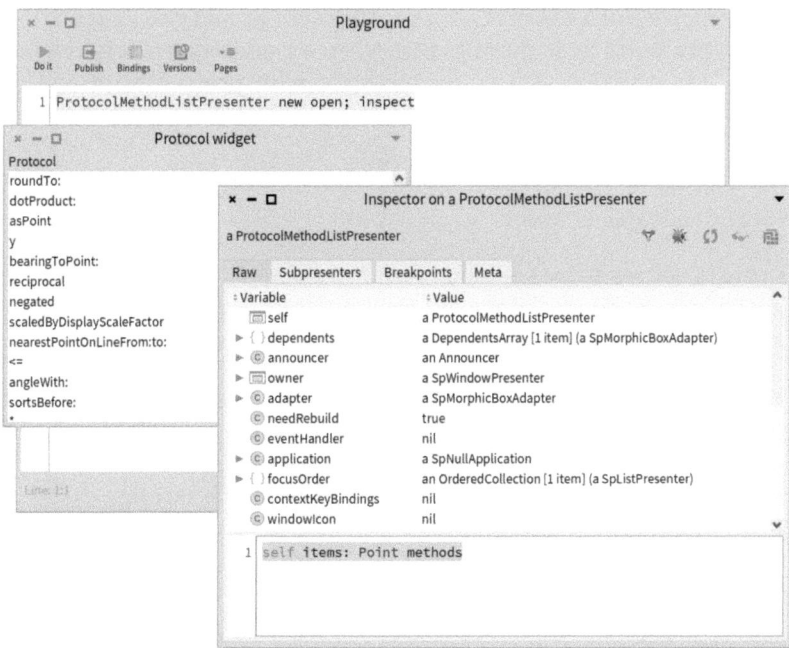

Figure 7-5 Live coding your widgets.

```
ProtocolMethodListPresenterTest >> testItems

    | proto methods |
    methods := Point methods sort: #selector ascending.
    proto := ProtocolMethodListPresenter new.
    proto items: methods.
    self assert: proto methods items first class equals: CompiledMethod.
    self assert: proto methods items first selector equals: methods
        first selector
```

We hope that we convinced you that writing simple UI tests is easy with Spec. Do not miss this opportunity to control the complexity of your software.

7.7 Managing three widgets and their interactions

The third user interface we build is a composition of the two previous user interfaces. We will see that there is no difference between configuring custom UIs and configuring system widgets: both kinds of widgets are configured by calling methods of the 'api' protocol.

Reuse and composition at work

This UI is composed of a `WidgetClassListPresenter` and two `ProtocolMethodListPresenters`. It specifies that when a model class is selected in the `WidgetClassListPresenter`, the methods in the protocols 'api' and 'api-events' will be shown in the two `ProtocolMethodListPresenter` widgets.

```
SpPresenter << #ProtocolViewerPresenter
  slots: { #models . #api . #events };
  package: 'CodeOfSpec20Book'
```

The `initializePresenters` method shows the use of `instantiate:` to instantiate widgets, and some of the different parameterization methods of the `ProtocolMethodListPresenter` class.

```
ProtocolViewerPresenter >> initializePresenters

  models := self instantiate: WidgetClassListPresenter.
  api := self instantiate: ProtocolMethodListPresenter.
  events := self instantiate: ProtocolMethodListPresenter.

  api label: 'api'.
  events label: 'api-events'.

  self focusOrder
    add: models;
    add: api;
    add: events
```

```
ProtocolViewerPresenter >> initializeWindow: aWindowPresenter

  aWindowPresenter title: 'Protocol viewer'
```

To describe the interactions between the different widgets we define the `connectPresenters` method. It specifies that when a class is selected, the selections in the method lists are reset and both method lists are populated. Additionally, when a method is selected in one method list, the selection in the other list is reset.

```
ProtocolViewerPresenter >> connectPresenters

  models whenSelectionChangedDo: [ :selection |
    | class |
    api resetSelection.
    events resetSelection.
    class := selection selectedItem.
    class
      ifNil: [
        api items: #().
        events items: #() ]
      ifNotNil: [
```

76

7.7 Managing three widgets and their interactions

```
            api items: (self methodsIn: class for: 'api').
            events items: (self methodsIn: class for: 'api - events') ] ].

  api whenSelectionChangedDo: [ :selection |
    selection selectedItem ifNotNil: [ events resetSelection ] ].
  events whenSelectionChangedDo: [ :selection |
    selection selectedItem ifNotNil: [ api resetSelection ] ]

ProtocolViewerPresenter >> methodsIn: class for: protocol

  ^ (class methodsInProtocol: protocol)
      sorted: [ :a :b | a selector < b selector ]
```

Lastly, the layout puts the subpresenters in one column, with all subpresenters taking the same amount of space.

```
ProtocolViewerPresenter >> defaultLayout

  ^ SpBoxLayout newTopToBottom
    add: #models;
    add: #api;
    add: #events;
    yourself
```

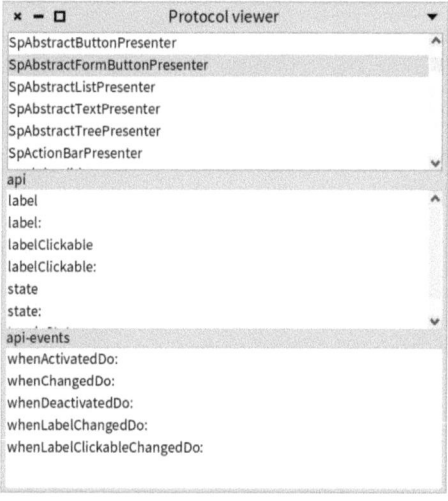

Figure 7-6 ProtocolViewerPresenter in vertical mode.

As previously, the result can be seen by executing the following snippet of code. The result is shown in Figure 7-6.

```
ProtocolViewerPresenter new open
```

This user interface is functional. Clicking on a class will show the methods of the 'api' and the 'api-events' protocols of that class.

7.8 Having different layouts

Note that you can change the layout as follows to get all the widgets in a row as shown in Figure 7-7. We will show later that a presenter can have multiple layouts and that the programmer decides which one to use.

We can do better. Let us define two methods as follows:

```
ProtocolViewerPresenter >> horizontalLayout

    ^ SpBoxLayout newLeftToRight
      add: #models;
      add: #api;
      add: #events;
      yourself
```

```
ProtocolViewerPresenter >> verticalLayout

    ^ SpBoxLayout newTopToBottom
      add: #models;
      add: #api;
      add: #events;
      yourself
```

```
ProtocolViewerPresenter >> defaultLayout

    ^ self verticalLayout
```

Now we can decide to open the viewer with different layouts using the message `openWithLayout:` as follows. See Figure 7-7 for the result.

```
ProtocolViewerPresenter class >> exampleHorizontal

    | inst |
    instance := self new.
    instance openWithLayout: instance horizontalLayout
```

7.9 Enhancing our API

Similar to the second user interface, when this UI is reused it will probably need to be configured. The relevant configuration here is what to do when a selection change happens in any of the three lists. Hence we add the following three methods to the 'api' protocol.

7.10 Changing the layout of a reused widget

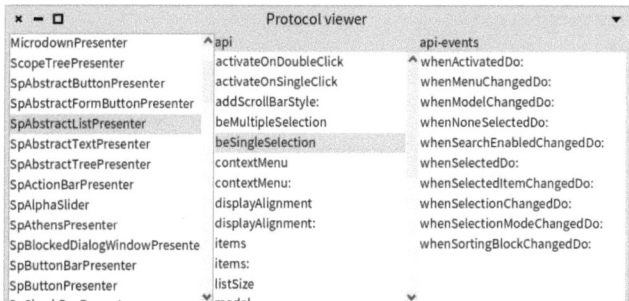

Figure 7-7 ProtocolViewerPresenter in horizontal mode.

```
ProtocolViewerPresenter >> whenSelectionInAPIChanged: aBlock
    api whenSelectionChangedDo: aBlock
```

```
ProtocolViewerPresenter >> whenSelectionInClassChanged: aBlock
    models whenSelectionChangedDo: aBlock
```

```
ProtocolViewerPresenter >> whenSelectionInEventChanged: aBlock
    events whenSelectionChangedDo: aBlock
```

Note. These methods add semantic information to the configuration API. They state that they configure what to do when a class, 'api', or 'api-events' list item has been changed. This arguably communicates the customization API more clearly than just having the subpresenters accessible.

7.10 Changing the layout of a reused widget

Sometimes, when you want to reuse an existing UI as a widget, the layout of that UI is not appropriate for your needs. Nonetheless Spec allows you to reuse such a UI by overriding the layout of its widgets, and we show this here.

Our last user interface reuses the `ProtocolViewerPresenter` with a different layout and adds a text zone to edit the source code of the selected method.

```
SpPresenter << #ProtocolCodeBrowserPresenter
    slots: { #text . #viewer };
    package: 'CodeOfSpec20Book'
```

Reuse and composition at work

```
ProtocolCodeBrowserPresenter >> initializePresenters

    text := self instantiate: SpCodePresenter.
    viewer := self instantiate: ProtocolViewerPresenter.
    text syntaxHighlight: true.
    self focusOrder
        add: viewer;
        add: text
```

```
ProtocolCodeBrowserPresenter >> defaultLayout

    ^ SpBoxLayout newTopToBottom
        add: (SpBoxLayout newLeftToRight add: #viewer; yourself);
        add: #text;
        yourself
```

```
ProtocolCodeBrowserPresenter >> initializeWindow: aWindowPresenter

    aWindowPresenter title: 'Spec Protocol Browser'
```

The connectPresenters method is used to make the text zone react to a selection in the lists. When a method is selected, the text zone updates its contents to show the source code of the selected method.

```
ProtocolCodeBrowserPresenter >> connectPresenters

    viewer whenSelectionInClassChanged: [ :selection |
        text behavior: selection selectedItem ].
    viewer whenSelectionInAPIChanged: [ :selection |
        selection selectedItem
            ifNotNil: [ :item | text beForMethod: item; text: item
        sourceCode ] ].
    viewer whenSelectionInEventChanged: [ :selection |
        selection selectedItem
            ifNotNil: [ :item | text beForMethod: item; text: item
        sourceCode ] ]
```

With the current implementation of initializePresenters, opening a window with ProtocolCodeBrowserPresenter new open results in a vertical layout for the ProtocolViewerPresenter instance held in the viewer instance variable because its default layout is the vertical layout. Our objective was to use a different layout. That can be achieved by sending layout: to the viewer. So let's adapt initializePresenters that way.

```
initializePresenters

    text := self instantiate: SpCodePresenter.
    viewer := self instantiate: ProtocolViewerPresenter.
    viewer layout: viewer horizontalLayout.
```

```
  text syntaxHighlight: true.
self focusOrder
  add: viewer;
  add: text
```

Now a window opens as shown in Figure 7-1.

7.11 Changing layouts

There are different ways to configure the layout of a presenter. Let's demonstrate that with `ProtocolViewerPresenter`. The first option is using `openWithLayout:` to open a window.

```
presenter := ProtocolViewerPresenter new.
presenter openWithLayout: (SpBoxLayout newLeftToRight
  add: #models;
  add: #api;
  add: #events;
  yourself)
```

Or you can send the message `layout:` to the presenter to specify a layout and open the window afterwards.

```
presenter := ProtocolViewerPresenter new.
presenter layout: (SpBoxLayout newLeftToRight
  add: #models;
  add: #api;
  add: #events;
  yourself).
presenter open
```

An alternative is to use a layout provided by the presenter, like we did in the previous section.

```
presenter := ProtocolViewerPresenter new.
presenter layout: presenter horizontalLayout.
presenter open
```

7.12 Considerations about a public configuration API

In this chapter, we have seen several definitions of methods in the public configuration API of the presenter being built. The implementation of our configuration methods is simply delegated to internal widgets, but a configuration can of course be more complex than that, depending on the internal logic of the UI.

For methods that simply delegate to the internal widgets, the question is whether it makes sense to define these as methods in the 'api' protocols at all. Fundamentally this is a design decision to be made by the programmer. Not having such methods makes the implementation of the presenter more lightweight but comes at the cost of less clear intent and of breaking encapsulation.

For the former cost, we have seen an example in the protocol method list of Section 7.4. The presence of the three methods defined there communicates to the user that we care about what to do when a class, 'api' or 'api-events' list item has been changed. Fundamentally the same also holds for the other examples in this chapter: each method in an 'api' protocol communicates an intent to the reuser: this is how we expect that this presenter will be configured. Without such declared methods, it is less clear to the reuser what can be done to effectively reuse a presenter.

For the latter cost, expecting reusers of the widget to directly send messages to internal objects (in instance variables) means breaking encapsulation. As a consequence, we are no longer free to change the internals of the UI, e.g., by renaming the instance variables to a better name or changing the kind of widget used. Such changes may break reusers of the presenter and hence severely limit how we can evolve this presenter in the future. It is safer to define a public API and ensure in future versions of the presenter that the functionality of this API remains the same.

So in the end it is important to consider future reusers of your UI and the future evolution of your UI. You need to make a tradeoff between writing extra methods and possibly making reuse of the UI harder as well as possibly making future evolution of the UI harder.

7.13 New versus old patterns

In Spec 1.0, list presenters exposed a different API, namely whenSelectedItemChanged:, as in the following example.

```
initializePresenters

    models := self instantiate: WidgetClassListPresenter.
    api := self instantiate: ProtocolMethodListPresenter.
    events := self instantiate: ProtocolMethodListPresenter.

    api label: 'api'.
    events label: 'api-events'


connectPresenters

    api whenSelectedItemChanged: [ :method |
        method ifNotNil: [ events resetSelection ] ].
```

```
events whenSelectedItemChanged: [ :method |
    method ifNotNil: [ api resetSelection ] ]
```

In Spec 2.0, list presenters and friends expose a different object that represents the selection of the list. The design rationale is that a selection is a complex object (single selection, multiple selection). So we have:

```
connectPresenters
  api whenSelectionChangedDo: [ :selection |
    selection selectedItem ifNotNil: [ events resetSelection ] ].
  events whenSelectionChangedDo: [ :selection |
    selection selectedItem ifNotNil: [ api resetSelection ] ]
```

The question for your presenters is what is the API that you should expose to your users. If you like the Spec 1.0 way, that is still possible as shown below.

```
whenSelectedItemChangedDo: aBlock
  methods whenSelectionChangedDo: [ :selection |
    selection selectedItem ifNotNil: [ :item | aBlock value: item ] ]
```

But we advise using the Spec 2.0 way because it will give your presenters consistency with the core presenters of Spec and it will be easier to make them collaborate.

7.14 Conclusion

In this chapter, we have discussed a key point of Spec: the ability to seamlessly reuse existing UIs as widgets. This ability comes with no significant cost to the creator of a UI. The only thing that needs to be taken into account is how a UI can (or should) be customized.

The reuse of complex widgets at no significant cost was a key design goal of Spec because it is an important productivity boost for the writing process of UIs. The boost firstly comes from being able to reuse existing nontrivial widgets, and secondly because it allows you to structure your UI in coherent and more easily manageable subparts with clear interfaces. We therefore encourage you to think of your UI as a composition of such subparts and construct it modularly, to yield greater productivity.

CHAPTER 8

Lists, tables and trees

An important part of user interfaces is displaying lists of data. Such lists can be structured as tables, plain lists, but also trees supporting the nesting of data.

Spec provides three main presenters: `SpListPresenter`, `SpTreePresenter`, and `SpTablePresenter`. In addition, it offers `SpComponentListPresenter` which allows one to embed any presenter in a list. In this chapter, we present some of the functionality of these presenters.

8.1 Lists

Creating a list is as simple as instantiating a `SpListPresenter` and specifying a list of items that the list should display. The following script illustrates this and the result is shown in Figure 8-1.

```
SpListPresenter new
    items: Collection withAllSubclasses;
    open
```

We can change the header title of the list using the message `headerTitle:`. The header title can be hidden using the message `hideHeaderTitle`.

8.2 Controlling item display

By default a list item is displayed using the result of the `asStringOrText` message sent to the item. We can configure a list to apply a block to control the display of each item using the message `display:`. The following script configures

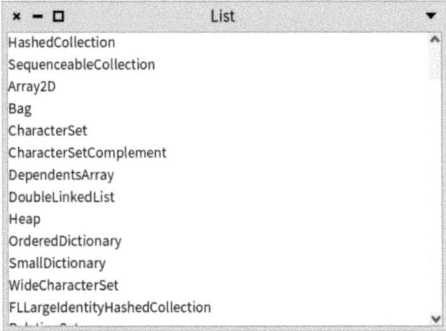

Figure 8-1 A simple list showing class names.

a list presenter to display the name of the methods of the class Point instead of showing the result of asStringOrText. See Figure 8-2.

```
SpListPresenter new
    items: Point methods;
    display: [ :item | item selector ];
    open
```

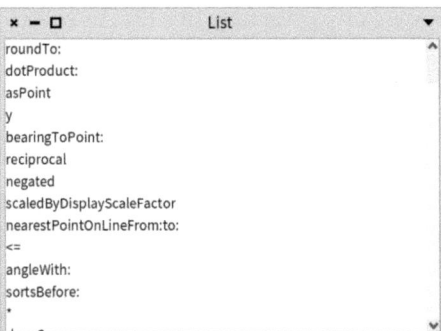

Figure 8-2 A simple list controlling the way items are displayed.

We can sort the items using the message sortingBlock:.

```
SpListPresenter new
    items: Point methods;
    display: [ :item | item selector ];
    sortingBlock: [ :a :b | a selector < b selector ];
    open
```

8.3 Decorating elements

We can configure the way items are displayed in a more fine-grained way. The following example illustrates it. We can control the icon associated with the item using the message `displayIcon:`, and the item color using the message `displayColor:`. The format (bold, italic, underline) can be controlled by the corresponding messages `displayItalic:`, `displayBold:` and `displayUnderline:`. See Figure 8-3.

```
SpListPresenter new
  items: Collection withAllSubclasses;
  displayIcon: [ :aClass | self iconNamed: aClass systemIconName ];
  displayColor: [ :aClass |
    (aClass name endsWith: 'Set')
      ifTrue: [ Color green ]
      ifFalse: [ self theme textColor ] ];
  displayItalic: [ :aClass | aClass isAbstract ];
  displayBold: [ :aClass | aClass hasSubclasses ];
  displayUnderline: [ :aClass | aClass numberOfMethods > 10 ];
  open
```

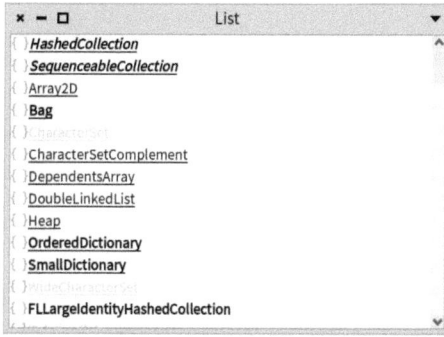

Figure 8-3 A decorated list: icons, text styling, and color.

8.4 About single/multiple selection

Lists support multiple selections. The message `beMultipleSelection` controls that aspect.

```
SpListPresenter new
  items: Collection withAllSubclasses;
  beMultipleSelection;
  open
```

Since selection can hold multiple items, there is an impact on the protocol to react to selection changes. Indeed, lists, filtering lists, trees, and tables offer the whenSelectionChangedDo: API and not whenSelectedItemDo:. The argument of the block is an instance of SpSingleSelectionMode, SpMultipleSelectionMode, SpTreeMultipleSelectionMode or SpTreeSingleSelectionMode.

Here is a typical use case of the method whenSelectionChangedDo:.

```
connectPresenters

  changesTree whenSelectionChangedDo: [ :selection | | diff |
    diff := selection selectedItem
      ifNil: [ '' ]
      ifNotNil: [ :item | self buildDiffFor: item ].
    textArea text: diff ]
```

8.5 Drag and drop

Lists and other container structures support drag and drop. The following script shows how to configure two lists to support dragging from one and dropping in another.

```
| list1 list2 |
list1 := SpListPresenter new.
list1
  items: #( 'abc' 'def' 'xyz' );
  dragEnabled: true.

list2 := SpListPresenter new.
list2 dropEnabled: true;
  wantsDrop: [ :transfer | transfer passenger
    allSatisfy: [:each | each isString ] ];
  acceptDrop: [ :transfer | list2 items: list2 items , transfer
    passenger ].

SpPresenter new
  layout: (SpBoxLayout newLeftToRight
    add: list1;
    add: list2;
    yourself);
  open
```

The following script illustrates the API.

- dragEnabled: configures the receiver to allow dragging of its items.
- dropEnabled: configures the receiver to accept dropped items.

- wantsDrop: [:transfer | transfer passenger allSatisfy: [:each | each isString]. With the message wantsDrop: we can specify a predicate to accept dropped elements.
- acceptDrop: [:transfer | list2 items: list2 items , transfer passenger]. The message acceptDrop: specifies the treatment performed once the dropped items are accepted.

8.6 Activation clicks

An element on a list can be *activated*, meaning it will trigger an event to execute an action on it. Note that an activation is different than a selection: one can *select* an element without activating it. The message activateOnDoubleClick configures the list to react to double click, while its counterpart is activateOnSingleClick.

8.7 Filtering lists

Lists can also be filtered as shown in Figure 8-4. The following script shows the use of the SpFilteringListPresenter.

```
SpFilteringListPresenter new
  items: Collection withAllSubclasses;
  open;
  withWindowDo: [ :window |
    window title: 'SpFilteringListPresenter example' ]
```

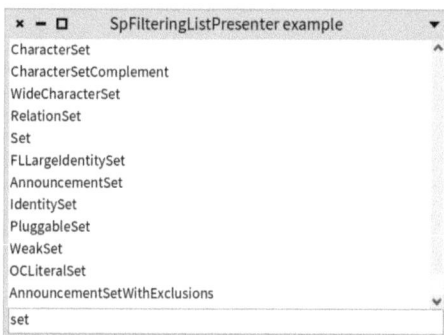

Figure 8-4 A filtering list with bottom filter.

The following script shows that the filter can be placed at the top.

Lists, tables and trees

```
SpFilteringListPresenter new
  items: Collection withAllSubclasses;
  openWithLayout: SpFilteringListPresenter topLayout;
  withWindowDo: [ :window |
    window title: 'SpFilteringListPresenter example' ]
```

Note that a filter can be declared upfront using the message `applyFilter:`.

```
SpFilteringListPresenter new
  items: Collection withAllSubclasses;
  openWithLayout: SpFilteringListPresenter topLayout;
  applyFilter: 'set';
  withWindowDo: [ :window |
    window title: 'SpFilteringListPresenter prefiltered example' ]
```

8.8 Selectable filtering lists

Often lists are used to select items. This is what the class `SpFilteringSelectableListPresenter` offers. In addition to being able to filter items, it lets the user select items by ticking them as shown by Figure 8-5.

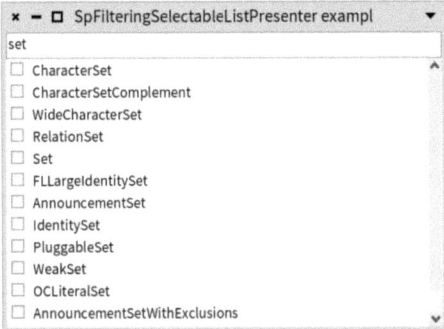

Figure 8-5 A selectable filtering list with a filter at the top.

The following script illustrates such a selectable list with filter.

```
(SpFilteringSelectableListPresenter new
  items: Collection withAllSubclasses;
  layout: SpFilteringListPresenter topLayout;
  applyFilter: 'set';
  asWindow)
    title: 'SpFilteringSelectableListPresenter example';
    open
```

8.9 Component lists

While the lists we saw until now are homogeneous in the sense that they all display strings, Spec offers the possibility to display a list of presenters. It means that elements in the list do not have the same size and can contain other presenters.

This lets developers produce advanced user interfaces such as the one of the report builder of the ModMoose tool suite shown in Figure 8-6.

Figure 8-6 An example of a component list from the ModMoose platform.

The following script shows how to define a `SpComponentListPresenter` as shown in Figure 8-7.

```
| list |
list := {
  (SpLabelPresenter new
    label: 'Test 1';
    yourself).
  (SpImagePresenter new
    image: (self iconNamed: #smallOk);
    yourself).
  (SpButtonPresenter new
    label: 'A button';
    yourself).
  (SpImagePresenter new
    image: PolymorphSystemSettings pharoLogo asForm;
    yourself) }.
```

```
SpComponentListPresenter new
  presenters: list;
  open
```

Figure 8-7 A component list with several different presenters: a label, an image, a button, and an image.

8.10 Trees

Spec offers also trees. The following script shows how to list all the classes of Pharo using inheritance as shown by Figure 8-8.

Figure 8-8 A Tree presenter showing the inheritance hierarchy of the class Exception.

```
SpTreePresenter new
  roots: { Object };
  children: [ :aClass | aClass subclasses ];
  displayIcon: [ :aClass | self iconNamed: aClass systemIconName ];
  display: [ :aClass | aClass name ];
  expandPath: #( 1 1 3 );
```

8.10 Trees

```
open
```

The message `expandPath:` shows that we can expand a specific item by a path.

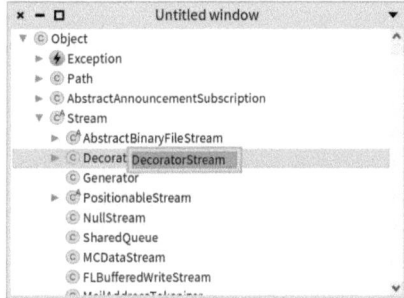

Figure 8-9   A tree with a menu.

The following script shows how to use a dynamic context menu. This is a dynamic menu because its content is recalculated. The dynamic aspect is expressed by a block. Figure 8-9 shows the result.

```
| tree |
tree := SpTreePresenter new.
tree roots: { Object };
  children: [ :aClass | aClass subclasses ];
  displayIcon: [ :aClass | self iconNamed: aClass systemIconName ];
  display: [ :aClass | aClass name ];
  contextMenu: [
    SpMenuPresenter new
      addGroup: [ :group |
        group addItem: [ :item | item name: tree selectedItem asString
    ] ] ];
  open
```

The following script shows the use of the message `selectPathByItems:scrollToSelection:`, which allows selecting elements by specifying a list of items (a path from the root to the selected item) and asking the tree to scroll to the selection. Figure 8-10 shows the result.

```
| pathToSpPresenter |
pathToSpPresenter := SpTreePresenter withAllSuperclasses reversed
    allButFirst.
SpTreePresenter new
  roots: { Object };
  children: [ :aClass | aClass subclasses ];
  displayIcon: [ :aClass | self iconNamed: aClass systemIconName ];
  display: [ :aClass | aClass name ];
```

Lists, tables and trees

```
open;
selectPathByItems: pathToSpPresenter scrollToSelection: true
```

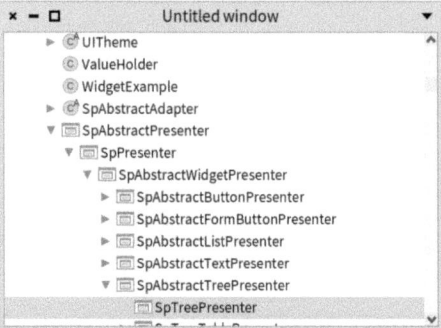

Figure 8-10 A tree with a selected item and scrolling to display it.

8.11 Tables

Spec offers tables. A table can have multiple columns and a column can be composed of elementary elements. Tables have different kinds of columns that can be added to a table:

- `SpStringTableColumn` offers cell items that are strings.
- `SpCheckBoxTableColumn` lets us have cells with a checkbox.
- `SpIndexTableColumn` displays the index of the current item.
- `SpDropListTableColumn` lets us have a drop list in cells.
- `SpImageTableColumn` offers cell items with forms (icons, graphics, ...).
- `SpCompositeTableColumn` offers the possibility to compose a column out of different kinds of columns. For instance, it allows one to compose an icon (`SpImageTableColumn`) with a name (`SpStringTableColumn`).

8.12 First table

The following script shows how to define a simple table with two columns as shown in Figure 8-11. The message `showColumnHeaders` will display the headers.

8.13 Sorting headers

```
SpTablePresenter new
   addColumn: (SpStringTableColumn title: 'Number' evaluated:
      #yourself);
   addColumn: (SpStringTableColumn title: 'Hex' evaluated: #hex);
   showColumnHeaders;
   items: (1 to: 10);
   open
```

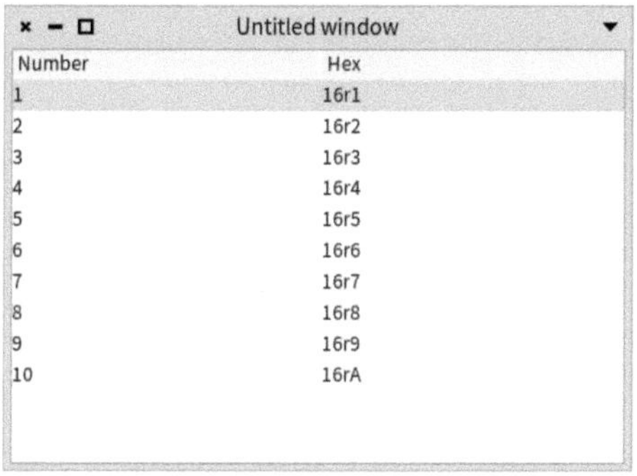

Figure 8-11 A simple table with two columns.

Add `SpIndexTableColumn title: 'My index'` to the previous table to see the index column in action.

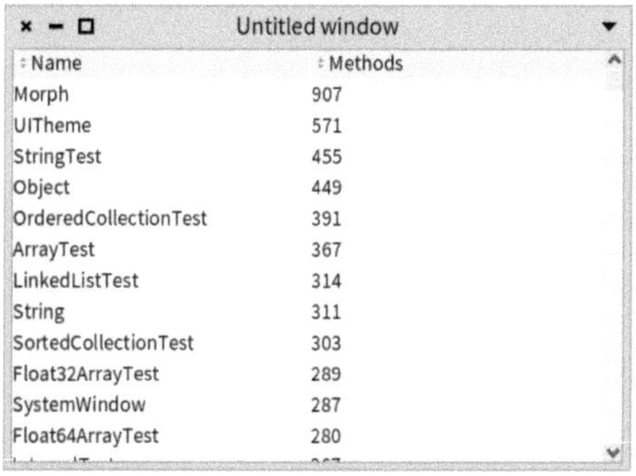

Figure 8-12 A simple table with two columns that can be sorted.

8.13 Sorting headers

The following script presents how to define a table with two sortable columns. Figure 8-12 shows the result after sorting the second column in descending

order.
```
| classNameCompare methodCountSorter |
classNameCompare := [ :c1 :c2 | c1 name < c2 name ].
methodCountSorter := [ :c1 :c2 |
  c1 methodDictionary size threeWayCompareTo: c2 methodDictionary size
    ].

SpTablePresenter new
  addColumn: ((SpStringTableColumn title: 'Name' evaluated: #name)
      compareFunction: classNameCompare);
  addColumn: ((SpStringTableColumn
      title: 'Methods'
      evaluated: [ :c | c methodDictionary size ]) sortFunction:
    methodCountSorter);
  items: Collection withAllSubclasses;
  open
```

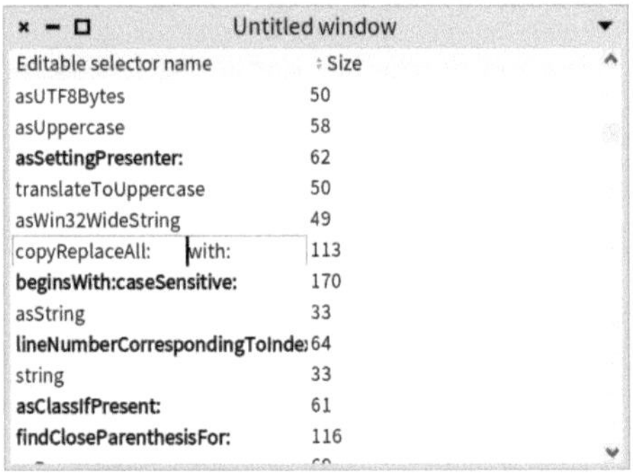

Figure 8-13 A table with an editable column.

8.14 Editable tables

The following script shows that table cells can be editable using the messages beEditable and onAcceptEdition:. The resulting table is shown in Figure 8-13.

```
| items |
items := String methods.
SpTablePresenter new
  addColumn:
    (SpStringTableColumn new
      title: 'Editable selector name';
      evaluated: [ :m | m selector ];
```

```
        displayBold: [ :m | m selector isKeyword ];
        beEditable;
        onAcceptEdition: [ :m :t |
          Transcript
            nextPutAll: t;
            cr;
            endEntry ];
      yourself);
    addColumn:
      (SpStringTableColumn title: 'Size' evaluated: #size)
        beSortable;
        showColumnHeaders;
        items: items;
    open
```

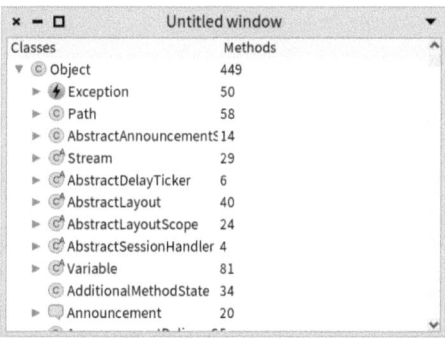

Figure 8-14 A tree table with two columns: the first one is a composed column with an icon and a string.

8.15 Tree tables

Spec offers a way to have a tree with extra columns. The class `SpTreeTablePresenter` encapsulates this behavior. Note that the first column is interpreted as a tree.

The following script shows that the first column will be a tree whose element is composed of an icon and a name: `SpCompositeTableColumn`. Figure 8-14 shows the window after expanding the root of the tree.

```
SpTreeTablePresenter new
  beResizable;
  addColumn:
    (SpCompositeTableColumn new
      title: 'Classes';
```

```
      addColumn:
        (SpImageTableColumn evaluated: [ :aClass |
           self iconNamed: aClass systemIconName ]);
      addColumn:
        (SpStringTableColumn evaluated: [ :each | each name ] );
      yourself);
   addColumn:
     (SpStringTableColumn new
        title: 'Methods';
        evaluated: [ :class | class methodDictionary size asString ]);
   roots: { Object };
   children: [ :aClass | aClass subclasses ];
   open
```

Sending the messages `width:` and `beExpandable` to the `SpCompositeTableColumn` instance fixes the size of the column.

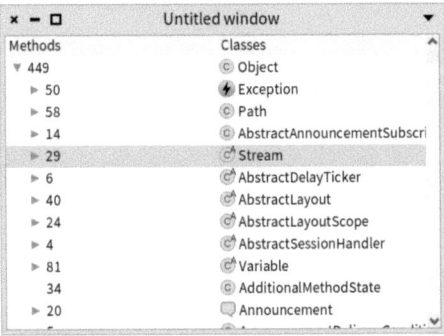

Figure 8-15 A tree table with two columns.

```
SpCompositeTableColumn new
  title: 'Classes';
  addColumn:
    (SpImageTableColumn evaluated: [ :aClass |
       self iconNamed: aClass systemIconName ]);
  addColumn: (SpStringTableColumn evaluated: #name);
  width: 250;
  beExpandable;
  yourself
```

You can try the following silly example which results in Figure 8-15.

```
| compositeColumn |
compositeColumn := SpCompositeTableColumn new title: 'Classes';
  addColumn: (SpImageTableColumn evaluated: [ :aClass |
       self iconNamed: aClass systemIconName ]);
```

```
    addColumn: (SpStringTableColumn evaluated: [ :each | each name ] );
    yourself.
SpTreeTablePresenter new
    beResizable;
    addColumn: (SpStringTableColumn new
        title: 'Methods';
        evaluated: [ :class | class methodDictionary size asString ]);
    addColumn: compositeColumn;
    roots: { Object };
    children: [ :aClass | aClass subclasses ];
    open
```

8.16 Conclusion

In this chapter, we presented important containers: list, component list, and table presenters.

CHAPTER 9

Managing windows

So far we have described the reuse of `SpPresenters`, discussed the fundamental functioning of Spec, and presented how to layout the widgets of a user interface. Yet what is still missing for a working user interface is showing all these widgets inside of a window. In our examples until now we have only shown a few of the features of Spec for managing windows, basically restricting ourselves to opening a window.

In this chapter, we provide a more complete overview of how Spec allows for the management of windows. We will show opening and closing, the built-in dialog box facility, the sizing of windows, and all kinds of window decoration.

9.1 A working example

To illustrate the window configuration options that are available, we use a simple `WindowExamplePresenter` class that has two buttons placed side by side. These buttons do not have any behavior associated yet. The behavior will be added in an example further down this chapter.

```
SpPresenter << #WindowExamplePresenter
    slots: { #minusButton . #plusButton };
    package: 'CodeOfSpec20Book'
```

```
WindowExamplePresenter >> initializePresenters

    plusButton := self newButton.
    minusButton := self newButton.
    plusButton label: '+'.
    minusButton label: '-'
```

Managing windows

Figure 9-1 A rather simple window on WindowExamplePresenter.

```
WindowExamplePresenter >> defaultLayout

    ^ SpBoxLayout newLeftToRight
        add: #plusButton;
        add: #minusButton;
        yourself
```

9.2 Opening a window or a dialog box

A user interface can be opened as a normal window or opened as a dialog box, i.e. without decoration and with 'Ok' and 'Cancel' buttons. We will show how this is done, including the configuration options specific to dialog boxes. See also Section 9.5 for more information about window decoration.

Opening a window

As we have shown in previous chapters, to open a user interface you have to instantiate the `SpPresenter` for that interface and send the `open` message to the instance. That results in the creation of an instance of `SpWindowPresenter` which points to the window containing the user interface, and showing it in a window on the screen.

We have also seen the `openWithLayout:` method that takes a layout (instance of SpLayout subclasses) as an argument. Instead of using the default layout, the opened UI will use the layout passed as an argument.

Below we show the two ways we can open a window for our `WindowExamplePresenter`. The code snippet opens two identical windows as shown in Figure 9-1.

9.2 Opening a window or a dialog box

```
| presenter |
presenter := WindowExamplePresenter new.
presenter open.
presenter openWithLayout: presenter defaultLayout
```

Opening a dialog box

Spec provides an easy way to open a UI as a simple dialog box with 'Ok' and 'Cancel' buttons. A dialog box does not have icons for resizing and closing, nor a window menu. To open a dialog box, send the message openDialog:

```
| presenter dialog |
presenter := WindowExamplePresenter new.
dialog := presenter openDialog
```

The answer of sending openDialog, assigned to the dialog variable above, is an instance of the SpDialogWindowPresenter class (a subclass of SpWindowPresenter). Figure 9-2 shows the dialog.

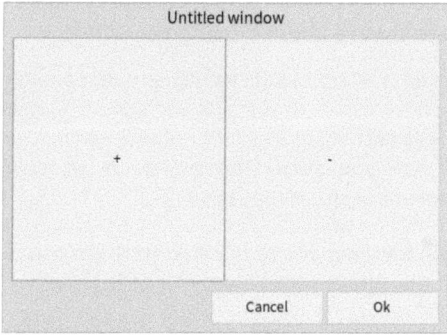

Figure 9-2 A rather simple dialog on WindowExamplePresenter.

The SpDialogWindowPresenter instance can be configured in multiple ways. To execute code when the user clicks on a button, send it the okAction: or cancelAction: message with a zero-argument block.

```
| presenter dialog |
presenter := WindowExamplePresenter new.
dialog := presenter openDialog
  okAction: [ 'okAction' crTrace ];
  cancelAction: [ 'cancelAction' crTrace ]
```

The message canceled sent to dialog will return true if the dialog is closed by clicking on the 'Cancel' button.

103

9.3 Preventing window close

Spec provides a way to check if a window can effectively be closed when the user clicks on the close box. SpWindowPresenter>>whenWillCloseDo: takes a block that decides whether the window can be closed. We can change our WindowExamplePresenter as follows:

```
WindowExamplePresenter >> initializeWindow: aWindowPresenter

    aWindowPresenter whenWillCloseDo: [ :announcement |
        announcement denyClose ]
```

The block has an announcement argument. It will be bound to an instance of SpWindowWillClose. That class has two interesting methods: allowClose and denyClose. The code snippet above sends denyClose to the announcement. By doing so, we have effectively created an unclosable window!

To be able to close this window, we have to change the implementation of the above method. By default a window can be closed, so the block should only send denyClose in case the window cannot be closed. Let's adapt the block to ask whether the user is sure about closing the window.

```
WindowExamplePresenter >> initializeWindow: aWindowPresenter

    aWindowPresenter whenWillCloseDo: [ :announcement |
        (self confirm: 'Are you sure that you want to close the window?')
            ifFalse: [ announcement denyClose ] ]
```

Of course, the example method above is extremely simplistic and not very useful. Instead, it should use application-dependent logic of what to check on window close.

9.4 Acting on window close

It is also possible to perform an action whenever a window is closed, both with a plain window or a dialog window.

With a window

When you want to be notified that a window is closed, you should redefine the initializeWindow: method in the class of your presenter as follows:

```
WindowExamplePresenter >> initializeWindow: aWindowPresenter

    aWindowPresenter whenClosedDo: [ self inform: 'When closed' ]
```

The following snippet programmatically opens and closes a window and you should see the notification triggered on close.

```
| presenter window |
presenter := WindowExamplePresenter new.
window := presenter open.
window close
```

With a dialog window

When you want the same behavior with a dialog window you can either use the mechanism as described previously (i.e. declare your interest in window closing in the method initializeWindow:) or configure the dialog presenter returned by the message openDialog.

```
| presenter dialog |
presenter := WindowExamplePresenter new.
dialog := presenter openDialog.
dialog
  okAction: [ 'okAction' crTrace ];
  cancelAction: [ 'cancelAction' crTrace ];
  whenClosedDo: [ self inform: 'Bye bye!' ]
```

Action with Window

The message withWindowDo: makes sure that the presenter that scheduled the window still exists or is in a state that makes sense.

```
[withWindowDo: [ :window | window title: 'MyTitle' ]
```

9.5 Window size and decoration

Now we focus on sizing a window before and after opening it, and then describe removing the different control widgets that decorate the window.

Setting initial size and changing size

To set the initial size of a window when it opens, send the initialExtent: message to the corresponding SpWindowPresenter before opening, for example like this:

```
| windowPresenter |
windowPresenter := WindowExamplePresenter new asWindow.
windowPresenter initialExtent: 300@80.
windowPresenter open
```

The common way to specify the initial size of the window is to use the message `initialExtent:` as follows:

```
WindowExamplePresenter >> initializeWindow: aWindowPresenter

    aWindowPresenter initialExtent: 80@100
```

Note that you can also set an initial position using the message `initialPosition:`.

After a window is opened, it can also be resized by sending the `resize:` message to the window of the UI. For example, we can change our example's `initializePresenters` method so that the window resizes itself depending on which button is clicked.

```
WindowExamplePresenter >> initializePresenters

    plusButton := self newButton.
    minusButton := self newButton.
    plusButton label: '+'.
    minusButton label: '-'.
    plusButton action: [ self window resize: 500@200 ].
    minusButton action: [ self window resize: 200@100 ]
```

You have also `centered`, `centeredRelativeTo:` and `centeredRelativeToTopWindow` to help you place the windows relative to world/other windows.

Fixed size

The size of a window can be fixed, so that the user cannot resize it by dragging the sides or corners as follows:

```
| presenter |
presenter := WindowExamplePresenter new open.
presenter window beUnresizeable
```

Removing window decoration

Sometimes it makes sense to have a window without decoration, i.e. without control widgets. Currently, this configuration cannot be performed on the SpWindowPresenter of that window, but the underlying widget library may allow it. Below we show how to get the SpWindow of our example and instruct it to remove the different control widgets:

```
| presenter |
presenter := WindowExamplePresenter new open.
presenter window
    removeCollapseBox;
    removeExpandBox;
```

9.5 Window size and decoration

```
removeCloseBox;
removeMenuBox
```

> **Note** This window is still closable using the halo menus or by calling `close` on the `SpWindowPresenter` instance (`presenter` in the example above).

Setting and changing the title

By default, the title of a new window is 'Untitled window'. Of course, this can be changed. The first way is to specialize the method `initializeWindow:` to send the message `title:` to the `windowPresenter` as follows:

```
WindowExamplePresenter >> initializeWindow: aWindowPresenter

    aWindowPresenter title: 'Click to grow or shrink.'
```

In addition, you can set the title of any UI after it has been opened (even if it specifies a `title` method) by sending the `title:` message with the new title as an argument to the window of the UI. An example is:

```
| presenter |
presenter := WindowExamplePresenter new.
presenter open.
presenter window title: 'I am different!'
```

Setting the about text

The about text of a window can be used by application developers to give a description of the application, and to list its contributors. The about text can be opened by selecting 'About' from the pop-up menu in the top-right corner of a window, as shown in Figure 9-3.

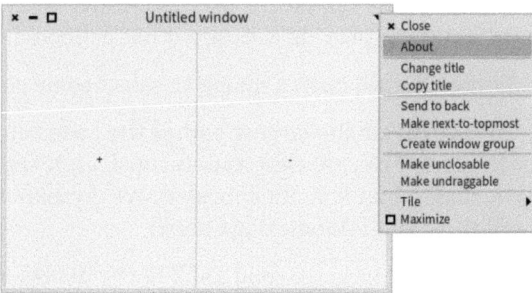

Figure 9-3 Opening the about text of a window.

Managing windows

To set the about text of a window, either override the aboutText method of the corresponding SpPresenter so that it returns the new about text, or send the instance the aboutText: message before opening, for example as below.

```
| windowPresenter |
windowPresenter := WindowExamplePresenter new asWindow.
windowPresenter aboutText: 'Click + to grow, - to shrink.'.
windowPresenter open
```

After opening the window with the code snippet above, and after choosing 'About' from the window menu, the about window opens with the configured about text, as shown in Figure 9-4.

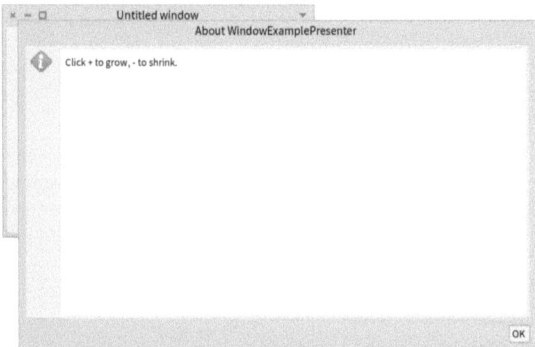

Figure 9-4 The about text of a window.

9.6 Getting values from a dialog window

Sending the message openDialog to a presenter will return the dialog window itself so that you can easily send it the message isOk. When isOk answers true, the dialog is in a state to provide the data it has collected from the user.

Let's look at an example. We will open a dialog to select some colors.

Configuring the UI makes up for the largest part of the code below, but the interesting part is at the end. The canceled state is the default state of a dialog so we have to tell the dialog that it is not canceled. We do that in the okAction block, where the dialog receives the message beOk.

Then in the whenClosedDo: block, we send isOk to the dialog. If that message answers true, it makes sense to process the selection of colors. For the sake of simplicity of this example, we just inspect the selected colors.

```
| selectedColors presenter colorTable dialogPresenter |
selectedColors := Set new.
presenter := SpPresenter new.
colorTable := presenter newTable
  items: (Color red wheel: 10);
  addColumn: (SpCheckBoxTableColumn new
    evaluated: [ :color | selectedColors includes: color ];
    onActivation: [ :color | selectedColors add: color];
    onDeactivation: [ :color | selectedColors remove: color];
    width: 20;
    yourself);
  addColumn: (SpStringTableColumn new
    evaluated: [ :color | '' ];
    displayBackgroundColor: [ :color | color ];
    yourself);
  hideColumnHeaders;
  yourself.
presenter layout: (SpBoxLayout newTopToBottom
  add: colorTable;
  yourself).
dialogPresenter := presenter openDialog.
dialogPresenter
  title: 'Select colors';
  okAction: [ :dialog | dialog beOk ];
  whenClosedDo: [ dialogPresenter isOk
    ifTrue: [ selectedColors inspect ] ]
```

9.7 Little modal dialog presenters

A modal dialog is a window that takes control of the entire Pharo user interface, making it impossible for the user to select another window while it is open.

Spec provides some little predefined dialogs to inform or request information from the users. Most of them inherit from `SpDialogPresenter`. They offer a builder API to configure them.

The simplest dialog is an alert.

```
SpAlertDialog new
  title: 'Inform example';
  label: 'You are seeing an inform dialog!';
  acceptLabel: 'Close this!';
  openModal
```

Confirm dialogs are created as follows:

```
SpConfirmDialog new
    title: 'Confirm example';
    label: 'Are you sure?';
    acceptLabel: 'Sure!';
    cancelLabel: 'No, forget it';
    onAccept: [ :dialog| dialog alert: 'Yes!' ];
    onCancel: [ :dialog| dialog alert: 'No!' ];
    openModal
```

The idiomatic way to use them is to access them via the application of your presenter class:

```
self application newAlert
    title: 'Inform example';
    label: 'You are seeing an inform dialog!';
    acceptLabel: 'Close this!';
    openModal
```

SpApplication offers the following API: newConfirm, newAlert, newJobList, newRequest, newSelect, newRequestText.

9.8 Placing a presenter inside a dialog window

Any presenter can be placed in a dialog window by specializing the method SpAbstractPresenter>>initializeDialogWindow:, which is implemented like this:

```
WindowExamplePresenter >> initializeDialogWindow:
        aDialogWindowPresenter
    "Used to initialize the model in the case of the use into a dialog
        window.
     Override this to set buttons other than the default (Ok, Cancel)."

    aDialogWindowPresenter
        addButton: 'Cancel' do: [ :presenter |
            presenter triggerCancelAction.
            presenter close ];
        addDefaultButton: 'Ok' do: [ :presenter |
            presenter triggerOkAction.
            presenter close ]
```

Override this method to define how your presenter will behave when it is open in a dialog window.

9.9 Setting keyboard focus

Some widgets can take keyboard focus. All text editing widgets come to mind, but lists can also take keyboard focus. Buttons too. In principle, when a presenter responds to keyboard events, it is able to take keyboard focus.

Widgets indicate that they have keyboard focus, typically by displaying a light-blue border around them. Figure 9-1 shows that the plus button on the left has the keyboard focus. A widget takes keyboard focus when the user clicks the widget with the mouse, or by pressing the tab key.

By pressing the tab key, the user makes the keyboard focus move forward from widget to widget according to the keyboard focus order of the widgets. By pressing shift-tab, the focus moves backward according to the focus order. By default, the focus order is the same as the order in which widgets are added to a user interface. Sometimes that order is not the desired order. In that case, the focus order has to be configured explicitly. A presenter can do that in the method `initializePresenters` by sending `focusOrder:` or by adding presenters to the answer of sending `focusOrder`. Let's try that in the `WindowExamplePresenter`.

```
WindowExamplePresenter >> initializePresenters

    plusButton := self newButton.
    minusButton := self newButton.
    plusButton label: '+'.
    minusButton label: '-'.
    self focusOrder
        add: minusButton;
        add: plusButton
```

Figure 9-5 shows the result after opening the window. The minus button has the keyboard focus.

9.10 Acting on window opening

Some state of presenters or their subpresenters can only be set after the window has been opened. That is the case when setting the state is delegated to the backend widgets. Those widgets are only available when the window is open. In Chapter 13, we will see that keyboard bindings for menu items in the menubar can only be assigned after opening the window. Here we will describe another use case, related to the previous section.

While defining the keyboard focus order does not require the window to be open, setting the initially focussed presenter does. Setting the initially focussed presenter is needed when the default keyboard focus order is not ap-

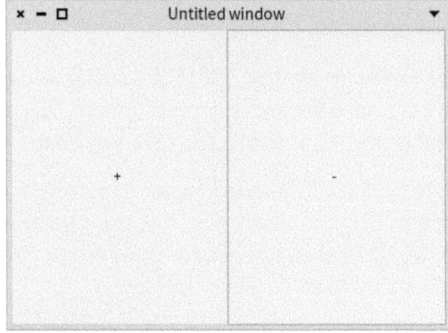

Figure 9-5   Reversed keyboard focus order.

propriate. That typically happens when using nested presenters that define a focus order, either implicitly or explicitly.

To demonstrate this, we will revert the method initializePresenters of WindowExamplePresenter from the previous section, and we will adapt initializeWindow:.

```
WindowExamplePresenter >> initializePresenters

    plusButton := self newButton.
    minusButton := self newButton.
    plusButton label: '+'.
    minusButton label: '-'
```

To set the initial keyboard focus on the minus button, we send takeKeyboardFocus to the presenter in the whenOpenedDo: block, which will be evaluated after opening the window.

```
WindowExamplePresenter >> initializeWindow: aWindowPresenter

    aWindowPresenter whenOpenedDo: [ minusButton takeKeyboardFocus ]
```

After opening the window, we see the keyboard focus on the minus button, as shown in 9-5.

We can go one step further. When opening an instance of WindowExamplePresenter in a dialog with WindowExamplePresenter new openDialog, the plus button has the keyboard focus because it is the first presenter in the default keyboard focus order. See Figure 9-2.

In case of a dialog, the initial keyboard focus on the plus button may not be desired. Probably it is more logical to put the keyboard focus on the Ok button of the dialog, so that the user can press the Enter key or the Space key to confirm the dialog immediately if no other interaction with the dialog is necessary. Let's do that. Instead of changing the method `initializeWindow:`, we change the method `initializeDialogWindow:`.

```
WindowExamplePresenter >> initializeDialogWindow:
    aDialogWindowPresenter

    super initializeDialogWindow: aDialogWindowPresenter.
    aDialogWindowPresenter whenOpenedDo: [ aDialogWindowPresenter
        defaultButton takeKeyboardFocus ]
```

aDialogWindowPresenter, which is bound to an instance of SpDialogWindowPresenter, understands the message defaultButton, which answers the Ok button. We send the message takeKeyboardFocus to the button. After opening the dialog with WindowExamplePresenter new openDialog, we see a dialog as shown in Figure 9-6, with the keyboard focus on the Ok button.

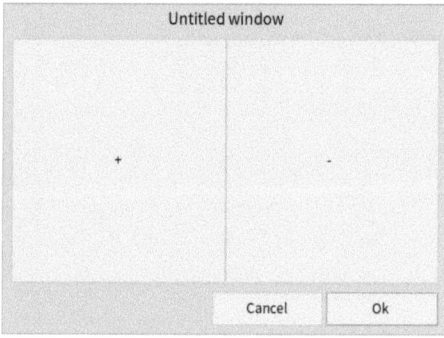

Figure 9-6 Keyboard focus on the Ok button of the dialog.

9.11 Conclusion

In this chapter, we treated the features of Spec that have to do with windows. First we described opening and closing windows as well as how to open a window as a dialog box. That was followed by configuring the window's size and its decorating widgets. After highlighting small yet important details of the window like its title and the about text, the chapter ended with handling dialogs.

CHAPTER 10

Layouts

In Spec, layouts are represented by instances of layout classes. The layout classes encode different positioning of elements such as box, paned, or grid. This chapter presents the available layouts, their definition, and how layouts can be reused when a presenter reuses other presenters.

10.1 Basic principle reminder

Spec expects that layout objects, instances of the layout classes, are associated with a presenter. Each presenter should describe the positioning of its subpresenters.

Contrary to Spec 1.0, where layouts were only defined at the class level, in Spec 2.0, to define the layout of a presenter you can:

- Define the `defaultLayout` method on the instance side
- Use the message `layout:` in your `initializePresenters` method to set an instance of layout in the current presenter.

The message `defaultLayout` returns a layout and `layout:` sets a layout, for example, an instance of `SpBoxLayout` or `SpPanedLayout`. These two methods are the preferred way to define layouts.

Note that the possibility of defining a class-side accessor e.g. `defaultLayout` remains for those who prefer it.

This new design reflects the dynamic nature of layouts in Spec, and the fact that you can compose them using presenter instances directly, not forcing you to declare subpresenters in instance variables upfront, and then use their names as it was done in Spec 1.0. It is, however, possible that there are cases where you want a layout "template"... so you can still do it.

10.2 A running example

To be able to play with the layouts defined in this chapter, we define a simple presenter named `TwoButtons`.

```
SpPresenter << #TwoButtons
    slots: { #button1 . #button2 };
    package: 'CodeOfSpec20Book'
```

We define a simple `initializePresenters` method as follows:

```
TwoButtons >> initializePresenters

    button1 := self newButton.
    button2 := self newButton.
    button1 label: '1'.
    button2 label: '2'
```

10.3 BoxLayout (SpBoxLayout and SpBoxConstraints)

The class `SpBoxLayout` displays presenters in an ordered sequence of boxes. A box layout can be horizontal or vertical and presenters are ordered left to right and top to bottom respectively. A box layout can be composed of other layouts.

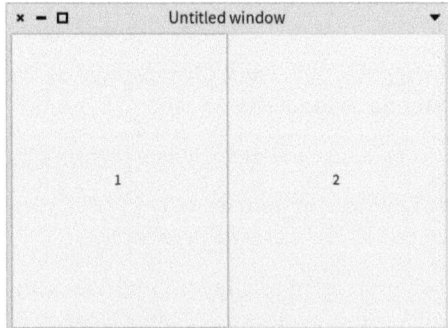

Figure 10-1 Two buttons placed horizontally from left to right.

Let us define a first simple layout as follows and whose result is displayed in Figure 10-1.

10.3 BoxLayout (SpBoxLayout and SpBoxConstraints)

```
TwoButtons >> defaultLayout

  ^ SpBoxLayout newLeftToRight
    add: button1;
    add: button2;
    yourself
```

What we see is that by default a subpresenter expands its size to fit the space of its container.

An element in a vertical box will use all available horizontal space, and fill vertical space according to the rules. This is inversed in a horizontal box.

We can refine this layout to indicate that the subpresenters should not expand to their container using the message add:expand:. The result is shown in Figure 10-2.

```
TwoButtons >> defaultLayout

  ^ SpBoxLayout newLeftToRight
    add: button1 expand: false;
    add: button2 expand: false;
    yourself
```

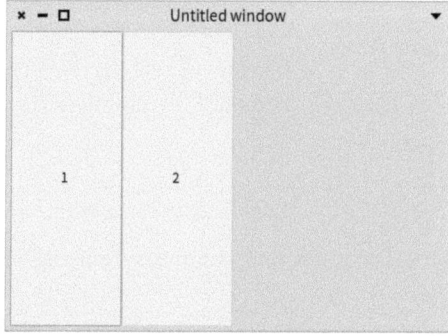

Figure 10-2 Two buttons placed from left to right, but not expanded.

The full message to add presenters is: add:expand:fill:padding:

- expand: argument - when true, the new child is to be given extra space allocated to the box. The extra space is divided evenly between all children that use this option.
- fill: argument - when true, the space given to a child by the expand option is actually allocated to the child, rather than just padding it. This parameter has no effect if expand is set to false.

- padding: argument - extra space in pixels to put between this child and its neighbors, over and above the global amount specified by the spacing property. If a child is a widget at one of the reference ends of the box, then padding pixels are also put between the child and the reference edge of the box.

To illustrate this API a bit, we change the defaultLayout method as follows. The result is shown in Fig 10-3. We want to stress, however, that it is better not to use a fixed height or padding.

```
TwoButtons >> defaultLayout

    ^ SpBoxLayout newTopToBottom
        spacing: 15;
        add: button1 expand: false fill: true padding: 5;
        add: button2 withConstraints: [ :constraints |
            constraints height: 80; padding: 5 ];
        yourself
```

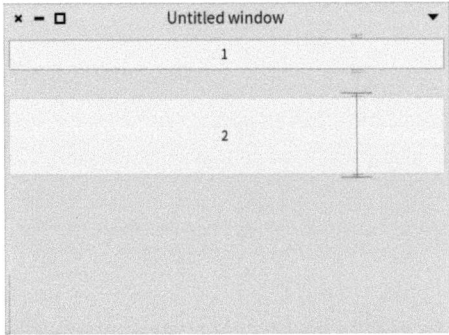

Figure 10-3 Two buttons placed from top to bottom playing with padding and fill options.

The annotations in the figure indicate the padding in red, the height of button2 in blue, and the spacing in green. Note that the padding of button2 is included in the height of the button.

The defaultLayout method sends the message withConstraints: [:constraints | constraints height: 80; padding: 5]. This message allows setting constraints when the often used messages add:, add:expand:, and add:expand:fill:padding: do not cover your particular use case. The constraints argument of the block is an instance of the SpBoxConstraints class.

10.4 Box layout alignment

A box layout can be configured with horizontal and vertical alignment of the children. These are the horizontal alignment options, which are messages that can be sent to a SpBoxLayout instance:

- hAlignStart
- hAlignCenter
- hAlignEnd

These are the vertical layout options:

- vAlignStart
- vAlignCenter
- vAlignEnd

10.5 Box alignment example

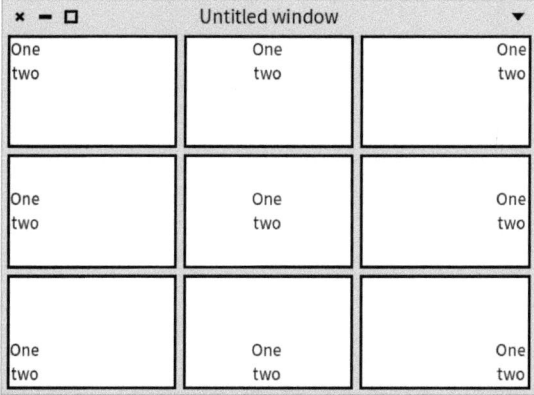

Figure 10-4 Nine tiles with different alignment options.

Let's see how this works in a small example as shown in Figure 10-4. We will create a presenter with 9 subpresenters, which we call "tiles", laid out in 3 rows with 3 columns. Each subpresenter displays two label presenters with the labels 'One' and 'Two'. The presenter class defines nine instance variables. The names refer to the position of the content inside each tile.

```
SpPresenter << #AlignmentExample
  slots: {
      #northWest .
      #north .
      #northEast .
      #west .
      #center .
      #east .
      #southWest .
      #south .
      #southEast };
  package: 'CodeOfSpec20Book'
```

As always, `initializePresenters` binds the instance variables that hold the subpresenters. It uses a helper method `newTile:` to create the tiles.

```
AlignmentExample >> initializePresenters

  northWest := self newTile: [ :tileLayout |
    tileLayout vAlignStart; hAlignStart ].
  north := self newTile: [ :tileLayout |
    tileLayout vAlignStart; hAlignCenter ].
  northEast := self newTile: [ :tileLayout |
    tileLayout vAlignStart; hAlignEnd ].
  west := self newTile: [ :tileLayout |
    tileLayout vAlignCenter; hAlignStart ].
  center := self newTile: [ :tileLayout |
    tileLayout vAlignCenter; hAlignCenter ].
  east := self newTile: [ :tileLayout |
    tileLayout vAlignCenter; hAlignEnd ].
  southWest := self newTile: [ :tileLayout |
    tileLayout vAlignEnd; hAlignStart ].
  south := self newTile: [ :tileLayout |
    tileLayout vAlignEnd; hAlignCenter ].
  southEast := self newTile: [ :tileLayout |
    tileLayout vAlignEnd; hAlignEnd ]
```

Note that the block argument of the `newTile:` message has a `titleLayout` argument, which is bound to an instance of `SpBoxLayout`. Inside the nine blocks, the alignment messages that we saw earlier are sent to configure the alignment inside the tiles. For instance, for the top-left tile called "northWest", `vAlignStart` is sent to align to the top side of the tile, and `hAlignStart` is sent to align to the left side of the tile.

```
AlignmentExample >> newTile: alignmentBlock

  | tileLayout |
  tileLayout := SpBoxLayout newTopToBottom
```

10.5 Box alignment example

```
    add: self newLabelOne;
    add: self newLabelTwo;
    yourself.
  alignmentBlock value: tileLayout.
  ^ SpPresenter new
    layout: tileLayout;
    addStyle: 'tile';
    yourself
```

The method `newTile:` uses two other helper methods:

```
AlignmentExample >> newLabelOne

  ^ self newLabel
    label: 'One';
    yourself
```

```
AlignmentExample >> newLabelTwo

  ^ self newLabel
    label: 'two';
    yourself
```

The layout of the window is defined with:

```
AlignmentExample >> defaultLayout

  ^ SpBoxLayout newTopToBottom
    spacing: 5;
    add: (self rowWithAll: { northWest . north . northEast });
    add: (self rowWithAll: { west . center . east });
    add: (self rowWithAll: { southWest . south . southEast });
    yourself
```

It answers a vertical box layout with three rows. It applies a spacing of 5 pixels between the rows. It sends `rowWithAll:` three times to create horizontal box layouts with three subpresenters each. `rowWithAll:` applies the same spacing of 5 pixels between the tiles in a row.

```
AlignmentExample >> rowWithAll: tiles

  | row |
  row := SpBoxLayout newLeftToRight
    spacing: 5;
    yourself.
  tiles do: [ :tile | row add: tile ].
  ^ row
```

For demonstration purposes, we apply a stylesheet to display tiles with a white background and a black border.

```
AlignmentExample >> application

    ^ SpApplication new
      addStyleSheetFromString: '.application [
        .tile [
          Container { #borderWidth: 2, #borderColor: #black },
          Draw { #backgroundColor: #white } ]
      ]';
      yourself
```

Now we have all the code we need to open the window with:

```
AlignmentExample new open
```

The result is shown in Figure 10-4. Each tile displays the label presenters at another location. The label presenters are positioned vertically.

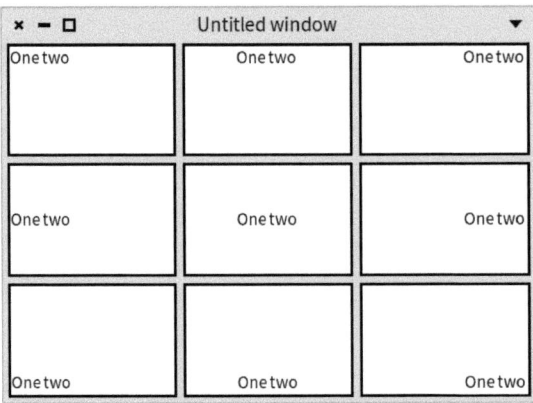

Figure 10-5 Nine tiles with the labels in a vertical box layout.

10.6 Alignment in horizontal box layout

Let's see what happens when we put the label presenters in a horizontal box layout.

```
AlignmentExample >> newTile: alignmentBlock

    | tileLayout |
    tileLayout := SpBoxLayout newLeftToRight
      add: self newLabelOne;
      add: self newLabelTwo;
```

10.7 A more advanced layout

```
    yourself.
  alignmentBlock value: tileLayout.
  ^ SpPresenter new
    layout: tileLayout;
    addStyle: 'tile';
    yourself
```

Figure 10-5 shows the result of opening the window again. Now the labels are positioned horizontally.

10.7 A more advanced layout

Now that we know how to align nested presenters, let's have a look at a common use case. Suppose we like to arrange three buttons in a row of which two are positioned on the left side of the window, and one is positioned on the right side. That setup is very handy for button bars with buttons on the left side and on the right side, such as in the Repositories browser of Iceberg, as you can see in Figure 10-6. The bar has one button on the left side and two buttons on the right side.

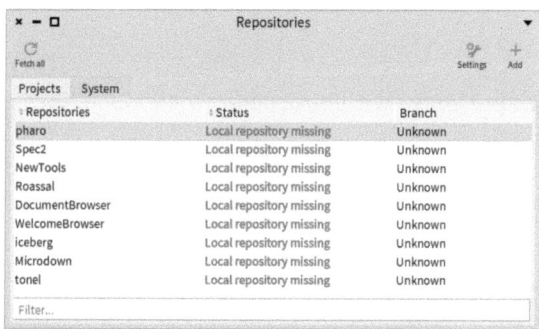

Figure 10-6 Buttons on the left side and on the right side.

Let's create a new presenter class called `ButtonBar`:

```
SpPresenter << #ButtonBar
  slots: { #button1 . #button2 . #button3 };
  package: 'CodeOfSpec20Book'
```

We initialize the three buttons:

```
ButtonBar >> initializePresenters

  button1 := self newButton.
  button2 := self newButton.
```

```
button3 := self newButton.
button1 label: '1'.
button2 label: '2'.
button3 label: '3'
```

We use a layout that has two sublayouts, one for two buttons on the left, and one for the third button on the right. We apply a 15 pixel spacing between the buttons on the left.

```
ButtonBar >> defaultLayout

    | left right |
    left := SpBoxLayout newLeftToRight
        spacing: 15;
        add: button1 expand: false;
        add: button2 expand: false;
        yourself.
    right := SpBoxLayout newLeftToRight
        add: button3 expand: false;
        yourself.
    ^ SpBoxLayout newLeftToRight
        add: left;
        add: right;
        yourself
```

When opening this presenter with `ButtonBar new open`, we see the window shown in Figure 10-7.

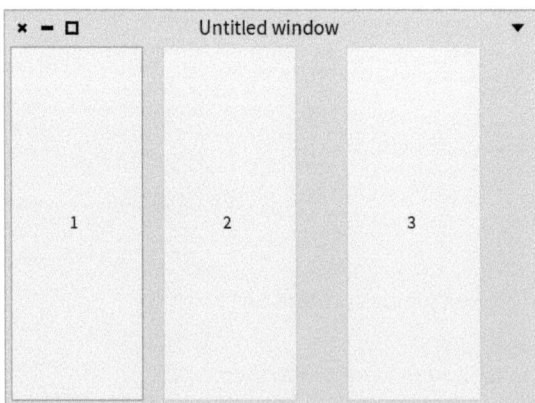

Figure 10-7 Three buttons split in a left and a right section.

The layout is not exactly what we had in mind. The third button is not positioned on the right side. That is where the alignment from the pevious section

10.7 A more advanced layout

comes in. Let's change the `defaultLayout` method to align the button with the end of the right box layout. We add the message `hAlignEnd`:

```
ButtonBar >> defaultLayout

  | left right |
  left := SpBoxLayout newLeftToRight
    spacing: 15;
    add: button1 expand: false;
    add: button2 expand: false;
    yourself.
  right := SpBoxLayout newLeftToRight
    hAlignEnd;
    add: button3 expand: false;
    yourself.
  ^ SpBoxLayout newLeftToRight
    add: left;
    add: right;
    yourself
```

When we open the presenter again, we see the window shown in Figure 10-8. That is the layout we had in mind.

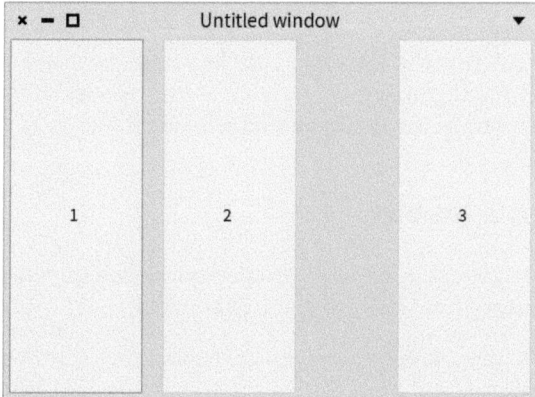

Figure 10-8 Three buttons with the third button aligned at the end.

This example shows that advanced layout requires nesting layouts to achieve the desired result.

125

10.8 Example setup for layout reuse

Before presenting some of the other layouts, we show an important aspect of Spec presenter composition: a composite can declare that it wants to reuse a presenter using a specific layout of a presenter.

Consider our artificial example of a two-button UI. Let us use two layouts as follows. We define two class methods returning different layouts. Note that we could define such methods on the instance side to. We define them on the class side to be able to get the layouts without an instance of the class.

```
TwoButtons class >> buttonRow

    ^ SpBoxLayout newLeftToRight
      add: #button1;
      add: #button2;
      yourself
```

```
TwoButtons class >> buttonColumn

    ^ SpBoxLayout newTopToBottom
      add: #button1;
      add: #button2;
      yourself
```

Note that when we define the layout at the class level, we use a symbol whose name is the corresponding instance variable. Hence we use #button2 to refer to the presenter stored in the instance variable button2.

10.9 Opening with a layout

The message openWithLayout: lets you specify the layout you want to use when opening a presenter. Here are some examples:

- TwoButtons new openWithLayout: TwoButtons buttonRow places the buttons in a row.
- TwoButtons new openWithLayout: TwoButtons buttonColumn places them in a column.

We define a defaultLayout method which invokes one of the previously defined methods so that the presenter can be opened without giving a layout.

```
TwoButtons >> defaultLayout

    ^ self class buttonRow
```

10.10 Better design

We can do better and define two instance level methods to encapsulate the layout configuration.

```
TwoButtons >> beColumn

    self layout: self class buttonColumn
```

```
TwoButtons >> beRow

    self layout: self class buttonRow
```

Then we can write the following script:

```
TwoButtons new
  beColumn;
  open
```

10.11 Specifying a layout when reusing a presenter

Having multiple layouts for a presenter implies that there is a way to specify the layout to use when a presenter is reused. This is simple. We use the method `layout:`. Here is an example. We create a new presenter named `ButtonAndListH`.

```
SpPresenter << #ButtonAndListH
  slots: { #buttons . #list };
  package: 'CodeOfSpec20Book'
```

```
ButtonAndListH >> initializePresenters

    buttons := self instantiate: TwoButtons.
    list := self newList.
    list items: (1 to: 10)
```

```
ButtonAndListH >> initializeWindow: aWindowPresenter

    aWindowPresenter title: 'SuperWidget'
```

```
ButtonAndListH >> defaultLayout

    ^ SpBoxLayout newLeftToRight
      add: buttons;
      add: list;
      yourself
```

This `ButtonAndListH` class results in a SuperWidget window as shown in Figure 10-9. It reuses the `TwoButtons` presenter and places all three presenters in a horizontal order because the TwoButtons presenter uses the buttonRow layout method by default.

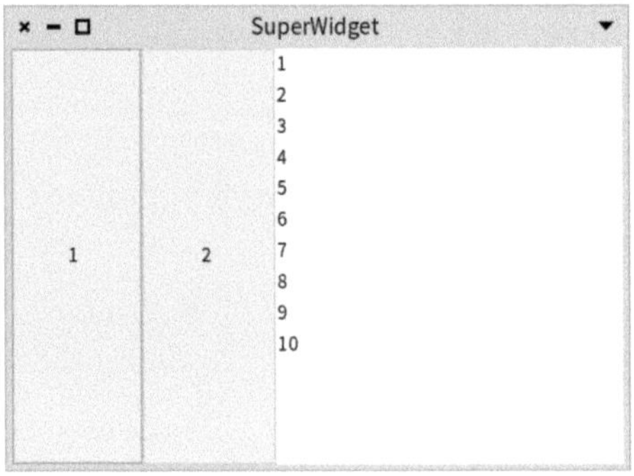

Figure 10-9 Buttons placed horizontally.

Alternatively, we can create ButtonAndListV class as a subclass of ButtonAndListH and only change the initializePresenters method as below. It specifies that the reused buttons widget should use the buttonColumn layout method, and hence results in the window shown in Figure 10-10.

```
ButtonAndListH << #ButtonAndListV
    slots: {};
    package: 'CodeOfSpec20Book'
```

```
ButtonAndListV >> initializePresenters

    super initializePresenters.
    buttons beColumn
```

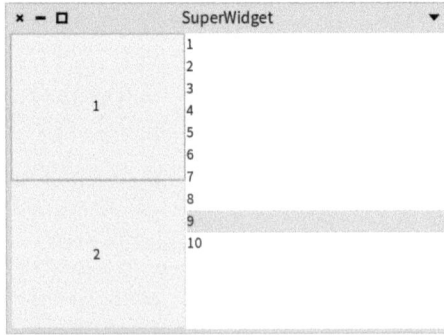

Figure 10-10 Buttons placed vertically.

10.12 Alternative to declare subcomponent layout choice

The alternative is to define a new method `defaultLayout` and to use the `add: layout:` message. We define a different presenter.

```
ButtonAndListH << #ButtonAndListV2
    slots: {};
    package: 'CodeOfSpec20Book'
```

We define a new `defaultLayout` method as follows:

```
ButtonAndListV2 >> defaultLayout

    ^ SpBoxLayout newTopToBottom
        add: buttons layout: #buttonColumn;
        add: list;
        yourself
```

Note the use of the message `add: layout:` with the selector of the method returning the layout configuration: `#buttonColumn`. This is normal since we cannot access the state of a subcomponent at this moment. Let's open a window with:

```
ButtonAndListV2 new open
```

That opens the window shown in Figure 10-11.

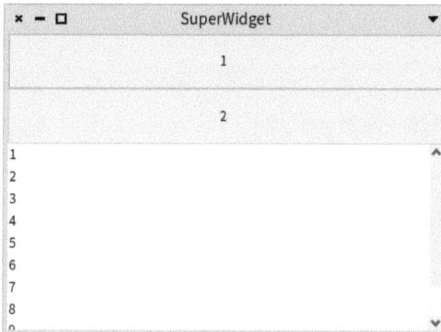

Figure 10-11 Buttons and list placed vertically.

10.13 Dynamically changing a layout

It is possible to change the layout of a presenter dynamically, for example from an inspector. Open the presenter with:

Layouts

```
[ ButtonAndListV new inspect open
```

That opens an inspector on the presenter, and a window with the buttons placed vertically as shown in Figure 10-10.

Then select the 'buttons' instance variable in the inspector and do `self beRow`. The result is shown Figure 10-12.

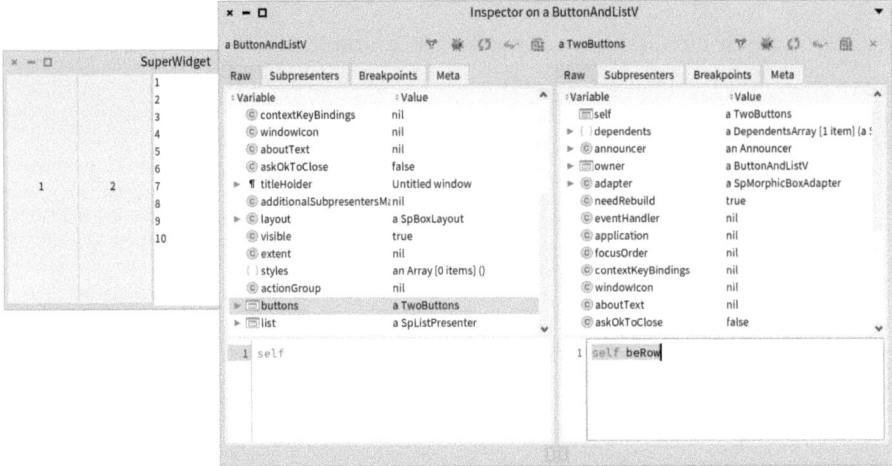

Figure 10-12 Tweaking and playing interactively with layouts from the inspector.

10.14 Grid layout (SpGridLayout)

The class `SpGridLayout` arranges subpresenters in a grid according to certain layout properties such as:

- A position that is mandatory (`columnNumber@rowNumber`) and
- A span that can be added if desired (`columnExtension@rowExtension`)

The following example opens a window with a grid layout with several widgets, as shown in Figure 10-13.

```
SpPresenter << #GridExample
    slots: { #promptLabel . #nameText . #suggestionsText . #submitButton
    };
    package: 'CodeOfSpec20Book'
```

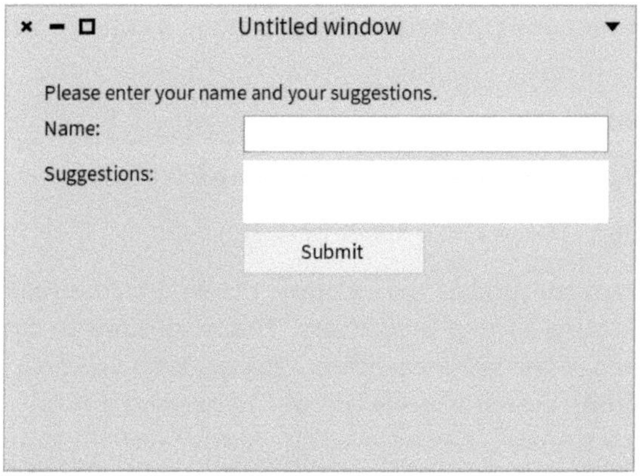

10.14 Grid layout (SpGridLayout)

Figure 10-13 A simple grid for a small form.

```
GridExample >> initializePresenters

  promptLabel := self newLabel
    label: 'Please enter your name and your suggestions.';
    yourself.
  nameText := self newTextInput.
  suggestionsText := self newText.
  submitButton := self newButton
    label: 'Submit';
    yourself
```

```
GridExample >> defaultLayout

  ^ SpGridLayout new
    add: #promptLabel at: 1@1 span: 3@1;
    add: 'Name:' at: 1@2;
    add: #nameText at: 2@2 span: 2@1;
    add: 'Suggestions:' at: 1@3;
    add: #suggestionsText at: 2@3 span: 2@1;
    add: #submitButton at: 2@4 span: 1@1;
    yourself
```

The layout defines a grid with three columns. The prompt 'Please enter your name and your suggestions.' spans the three columns. The labels of the two fields are put in the first column. The fields span the second and the third column. The button is put in the second column. The second field is a multi-line text field. That is why it is higher than the first field, which is a single-line text field.

Here is a list of options:

- `columnHomogeneous`: Whether presenters in a column will have the same size.
- `rowHomogeneous`: Whether presenters a row will have the same size.
- `colSpacing:`: The horizontal space between cells.
- `rowSpacing:`: The vertical space between cells.

The `defaultLayout` method of the example maybe hard to read, especially when the grid contains a lot of presenters. The reader has to compute the positions and the spans of the subpresenters. We can use a `SpGridLayoutBuilder` to make grid building easier. The class is not to be used directly. Instead send `build:` to a `SpGridLayout`. Below is an alternative `defaultlayout` method that produces the same result as before. By putting all presenters of one row on one line, it is clear that there are four rows, and it is clear which subpresenters are part of the same row.

```
GridExample >> defaultLayout

  ^ SpGridLayout build: [ :builder |
    builder
      add: #promptLabel span: 3@1; nextRow;
      add: 'Name:'; add: #nameText span: 2@1; nextRow;
      add: 'Suggestions:'; add: #suggestionsText span: 2@1; nextRow;
      nextColumn; add: #submitButton ]
```

10.15 Paned layout (SpPanedLayout)

A paned layout is like a box layout, but restricted to two children, which are the "panes". It places children in a vertical or horizontal fashion and adds a splitter in between, that the user can drag to resize the panes. The message `positionOfSlider:` indicates the original position of the splitter. It can be nil (then it defaults to 50%), or it can be a percentage (e.g. 70 percent), a `Float` (e.g. 0.7), or a `Fraction` (e.g. 7/10). We prefer simplicity and use floats because there are cheap and simple.

Let's look at this simple example:

```
SpPresenter << #PanedLayoutExample
  slots: { #leftList . #rightList };
  package: 'CodeOfSpec20Book'
```

```
PanedLayoutExample >> initializePresenters

  leftList := self newList
    items: (1 to: 10);
    yourself.
```

10.16 Overlay layout (SpOverlayLayout)

```
rightList := self newList
  items: ($a to: $z);
  yourself
```

```
PanedLayoutExample >> defaultLayout

  ^ SpPanedLayout newLeftToRight
    positionOfSlider: 0.7;
    add: #leftList;
    add: #rightList;
    yourself
```

Let's open the presenter with:

```
PanedLayoutExample new open
```

Figure 10-14 shows the result. The left list takes 70% of the width of the window and the right list takes 30%.

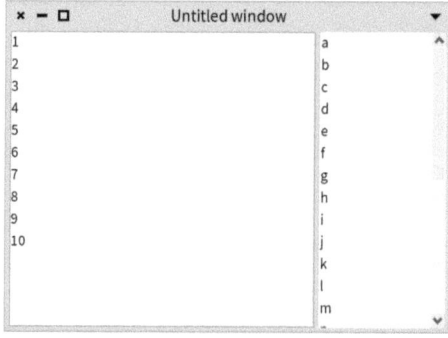

Figure 10-14 A paned layout with two lists.

10.16 Overlay layout (SpOverlayLayout)

An overlay layout allows overlaying one presenter by other presenters.

As an example, we will create a presenter that shows a button labeled 'Inbox', with a red indicator overlayed in the top-right corner (See Figure 10-15). A use case could be indicating that there are unread messages in the inbox.

```
SpPresenter << #OverlayLayoutExample
  slots: { #button . #indicator };
  package: 'CodeOfSpec20Book'
```

Layouts

Figure 10-15 An overlay layout with a button and a Roassal box.

The method `initializePresenters` creates the button and the indicator. The latter is a `SpRoassalPresenter`. We use a helper method to answer the shape that should be shown.

```
OverlayLayoutExample >> initializePresenters

  button := self newButton
    label: 'Inbox';
    yourself.
  indicator := (self instantiate: SpRoassalPresenter)
    script: [ :view | view addShape: self indicatorShape ];
    yourself
```

```
OverlayLayoutExample >> indicatorShape

  ^ RSBox new
      extent: 10@10;
      color: Color red;
      yourself
```

To make the structure of the layout clear, we have three methods. The defaultLayout is the layout of the window. For demonstration purposes, we put the button in the middle of the window. The button's dimensions are 50 by 50 pixels.

```
OverlayLayoutExample >> defaultLayout

  | buttonVBox |
  buttonVBox := SpBoxLayout newTopToBottom
      vAlignCenter;
      add: self buttonLayout height: 50;
      yourself.
```

134

10.16 Overlay layout (SpOverlayLayout)

```
^ SpBoxLayout newLeftToRight
    hAlignCenter;
    add: buttonVBox width: 50;
    yourself
```

The defaultLayout method sends the message buttonLayout to fetch the overlay layout for the button and the indicator. Let us define the method buttonLayout as follows:

```
OverlayLayoutExample >> buttonLayout

    ^ SpOverlayLayout new
        child: button;
        addOverlay: self indicatorLayout
            withConstraints: [ :constraints |
                constraints vAlignStart; hAlignEnd ];
        yourself
```

The child is the presenter that we want to overlay with the indicator. It is possible to add multiple overlays. In this example, we have only one, which is defined by indicatorLayout. Note that addOverlay:withConstraints: is used to configure where the overlay presenter should be displayed. We display it in the top-right corner, by sending vAlignStart (top) and hAlignEnd (right).

Now we define the method indicatorLayout as follows:

```
OverlayLayoutExample >> indicatorLayout

    | counterVBox |
    counterVBox := SpBoxLayout newTopToBottom
        add: indicator withConstraints: [ :constraints |
            constraints height: 12; padding: 2 ];
        yourself.
    ^ SpBoxLayout newLeftToRight
        add: counterVBox withConstraints: [ :constraints |
            constraints width: 12; padding: 2 ];
        yourself
```

The indicatorLayout method defines the layout for the indicator. To apply a vertical and a horizontal padding, we have to wrap a vertical box layout with a horizontal box layout. We could have wrapped a horizontal box layout with a vertical box layout to achieve the same result. We apply a padding of 2 pixels so that the indicator does not overlap the border of the button.

With all these methods in place, we can open the presenter.

```
OverlayLayoutExample new open.
```

That opens the window shown in Figure 10-15.

10.17 Conclusion

Spec offers several predefined layouts. Probably new ones will be added but in a compatible way. An important closing point is that layouts can be dynamically composed. It means that you are able to design applications that can adapt to specific conditions.

CHAPTER 11

Dynamic presenters

Contrary to Spec 1.0, in Spec 2.0 all the layouts are dynamic. It means that you can change the displayed elements on the fly. It is a radical improvement from Spec 1.0 where most of the layouts were static and building dynamic widgets was cumbersome.

In this chapter, we show that presenters can be dynamically composed using layouts. We show a little interactive session. Then we build a little browser with dynamic aspects.

11.1 Layouts as simple as objects

Building dynamic applications using Spec is simple. In fact, any layout in Spec is dynamic and composable. Let's explore how that works. We start with the following code snippet:

```
presenter := SpPresenter new.
presenter application: SpApplication new.
```

For this presenter, we use the `SpPanedLayout` which can receive two presenters (or layouts) and place them in one half of the window. If you want to see all the available layouts in Spec, you can check the package `Spec2-Layout`.

```
presenter layout: SpPanedLayout newTopToBottom.
presenter open.
```

Of course, as shown in Figure 11-1, we are going to see an empty window because we did not put anything in the layout.

Figure 11-1 An empty layout.

Now, without closing the window, we can dynamically edit the layout of the main presenter. We will add a button presenter by executing the following lines:

```
button1 := presenter newButton.
button1 label: 'I am a button'.
presenter layout add: button1.
```

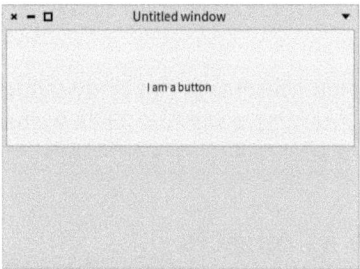

Figure 11-2 Paned layout with one button.

Now we can add another button. There is no need to close and reopen the window. Everything updates dynamically and without the need of rebuilding the window. As we have instantiated the layout with newTopToBottom, the presenters will be laid out vertically. See Figure 11-3.

```
button2 := presenter newButton.
button2 label: 'I am another button'.
presenter layout add: button2.
```

We can put an icon in the first button. See Figure 11-4.

```
button1 icon: (button1 iconNamed: #smallDoIt).
```

11.1 Layouts as simple as objects

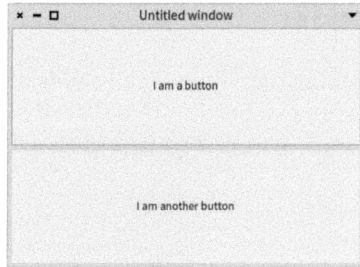

Figure 11-3 Paned layout with two buttons.

Figure 11-4 Paned layout with two buttons, one with an icon.

Or we can delete one of the buttons from the layout, as shown in Figure 11-5.

```
[presenter layout remove: button2.
```

Figure 11-5 Removing a button.

What you see here is that all the changes happen simply by creating a new instance of a given layout and sending messages to it. It means that programs can define complex logic for the dynamic behavior of a presenter.

11.2 Dynamic button adder

Now we will create a presenter that dynamically adds buttons with random numbers: we will add and remove buttons dynamically (as shown in Figures 11-6 and 11-7). Let us get started. We create a new class called `DynamicButtons`.

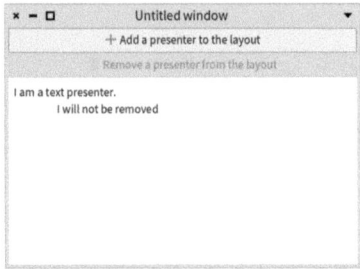

Figure 11-6 A presenter that dynamically adds buttons.

```
SpPresenter << #DynamicButtons
  slots: { #addButton . #removeButton . #text };
  package: 'CodeOfSpec20Book'
```

In the method `initializePresenters`, we add a button. When we click on it, it adds a new button to the layout. We also want a button that will remove the last button that was added, if any. Finally, we add a read-only text presenter that cannot be removed.

```
DynamicButtons >> initializePresenters

  addButton := self newButton.
  addButton
    action: [ self addToLayout ];
    label: 'Add a presenter to the layout';
    icon: (self iconNamed: #smallAdd).

  removeButton := self newButton.
  removeButton
    action: [ self removeFromLayout ];
    label: 'Remove a presenter from the layout';
    icon: (self iconNamed: #smallDelete);
    disable.

  text := self newText.
  text
    text: 'I am a text presenter.
I will not be removed';
```

```
beNotEditable
```

11.3 Defining add/remove buttons

Now we have to implement the methods `addToLayout` and `removeFromLayout` used in the action blocks of the buttons. Those methods, as their names indicate, add and remove presenters dynamically.

Let's start with the `addToLayout` method. We will add a new button to the layout. The label of the new button is a random number. We enable the remove button so that the newly added button can be removed.

```
DynamicButtons >> addToLayout

  | randomButtonName newButton |
  removeButton enable.
  randomButtonName := 'Random number: ', 1000 atRandom asString.
  newButton := self newButton
    label: randomButtonName;
    icon: (self iconNamed: #smallObjects);
    yourself.
  self layout add: newButton expand: false
```

For removing a button from the layout, we first check if there is a button that we can remove. If yes, we just remove the last button. Then, if there are no more buttons left to remove, we disable the remove button.

```
DynamicButtons >> removeFromLayout

  self layout remove: self layout presenters last.
  self layout presenters last = text ifTrue: [ removeButton disable ]
```

The only thing that is still missing is the default layout.

```
DynamicButtons >> defaultLayout

  ^ SpBoxLayout newTopToBottom
      add: addButton expand: false;
      add: removeButton expand: false;
      add: text;
      yourself
```

After opening the window with the following code snippet, we see the window shown in Figure 11-6.

```
DynamicButtons new open
```

Figure 11-7 shows what the window looks like after clicking the add button four times.

Dynamic presenters

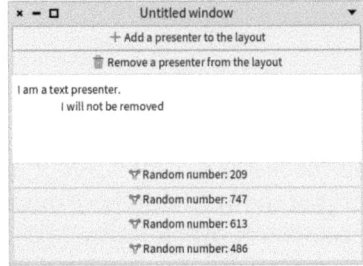

Figure 11-7 Adding random buttons.

11.4 Building a little dynamic browser

With all of the knowledge gained so far, we are going to build a new mini version of the System Browser as shown in Figure 11-8. We want to have:

- A tree that shows all the system classes.
- A list that shows all methods of the selected class.
- A text presenter that shows the code of a selected method.
- A button.

Initially, the code of the method will be in "Read-only" mode. When we press the button, we are switching to "Edit" mode.

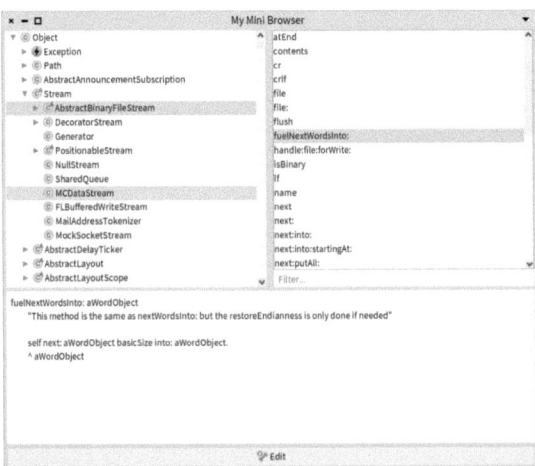

Figure 11-8 The mini browser in action.

11.4 Building a little dynamic browser

Let's get started.

```
SpPresenter << #MyMiniBrowser
    slots: { #classTree . #code . #methodList . #button };
    package: 'CodeOfSpec20Book'
```

The initializePresenters method instantiates the tree presenter class. We want the tree presenter to show all the classes that are present in the Pharo image. We know that (almost) all subclasses inherit from Object, so that is going to be the only root of the tree. To get the children of a tree node, we can send the message subclasses to a class. We want each of the tree nodes to have a nice icon. We can fetch the icon of a class with the message systemIconName. Finally, we want to "activate" the presenter with only one click instead of two.

```
MyMiniBrowser >> initializePresenters

    classTree := self newTree
        activateOnSingleClick;
        roots: { Object };
        children: [ :each | each subclasses ];
        displayIcon: [ :each | self iconNamed: each systemIconName ];
        yourself.
```

For the methods, we want to use a filtering list, so that we can search for method selectors. Also, we want to display only the selector of the method and sort the methods in an ascending way.

```
methodList := self newFilteringList
    display: [ :method | method selector ].
methodList listPresenter
    sortingBlock: [ :method | method selector ] ascending.
```

We said that, initially, the code is going to be in "Read-only" mode. The label of the button is going to be "Edit" to say that if we click on the button, we will change to "Edit" mode. We also want to have a nice icon.

```
button := self newButton
    label: 'Edit';
    icon: (self iconNamed: #smallConfiguration);
    yourself.
```

As the initial behavior will be read-only mode, the code will be a text presenter that is not editable.

```
code := self newText.
code beNotEditable
```

Here is the complete code of the method:

Dynamic presenters

```
MyMiniBrowser >> initializePresenters

    classTree := self newTree
        activateOnSingleClick;
        roots: { Object };
        children: [ :each | each subclasses ];
        displayIcon: [ :each | self iconNamed: each systemIconName ];
        yourself.
    methodList := self newFilteringList
        display: [ :method | method selector ].
    methodList listPresenter
        sortingBlock: [ :method | method selector ] ascending.
    button := self newButton
        label: 'Edit';
        icon: (self iconNamed: #smallConfiguration);
        yourself.
    code := self newText.
    code beNotEditable
```

Opening the presenter with the code below, opens the window shown in Figure 11-9.

```
MyMiniBrowser new open
```

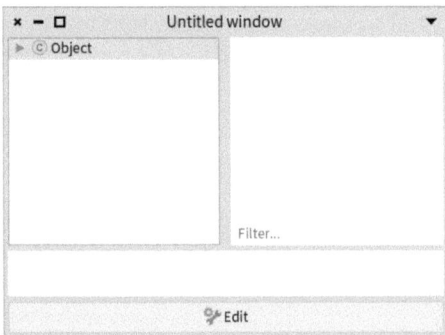

Figure 11-9 A little browser in read-only mode.

11.5 Placing elements visually

We initialized our presenters, but we did not indicate how they needed to be displayed.

We want the upper part of the layout to have the classes and the methods shown horizontally, like in the System Browser. To achieve that, we will create another left-to-right layout, with a spacing of 10 pixels between the classes and the methods.

We add that layout to our main layout, which is a top-to-bottom layout. We add the code and the button under the classes and the methods. We do not want the code to expand. In addition, we want a separation of 5 pixels for this layout.

```
MyMiniBrowser >> defaultLayout

    | classesAndMethodsLayout |
    classesAndMethodsLayout := SpBoxLayout newLeftToRight.
    classesAndMethodsLayout
        spacing: 10;
        add: classTree;
        add: methodList.
    ^ SpBoxLayout newTopToBottom
        spacing: 5;
        add: classesAndMethodsLayout;
        add: code;
        add: button expand: false;
        yourself
```

11.6 Connecting the flow

So far so good, but we did not add any behavior to the presenters. We have to implement the `connectPresenters` method.

When we click on a class in the tree, we want to update the items of the method list with the methods of the selected class. When we click on a method, we want to update the text of the code with the source code of the method.

```
MyMiniBrowserPresenter >> connectPresenters

    classTree whenActivatedDo: [ :selection |
        methodList items: selection selectedItem methods ].
    methodList listPresenter
        whenSelectedDo: [ :selectedMethod |
            code text: selectedMethod ast formattedCode ].
    button action: [ self buttonAction ]
```

For now, we define the method `buttonAction` to do nothing.

```
MyMiniBrowserPresenter >> buttonAction
```

11.7 Toggling Edit/Read-only mode

When we click on the button we want several things. That is why it is better to create a separate method.

1. We want to change the label of the button to alternate between "Edit" and "Read only".
2. We want to change the presenter of the code. If the Mini Browser is in read-only mode, we want to have a text presenter that is not editable. If the Mini Browser is in edit mode, we want to have a code presenter that applies syntax coloring to the code and shows the line numbers. But always the code is going to have the same text (the code of the selected method).

```
MyMiniBrowserPresenter >> buttonAction

    | newCode |
    button label = 'Edit'
      ifTrue: [
        button label: 'Read only'.
        newCode := self newCode
          beForMethod: methodList selectedItem;
          text: methodList selectedItem ast formattedCode;
          yourself ]
      ifFalse: [
        button label: 'Edit'.
        newCode := self newText
          text: methodList selectedItem ast formattedCode;
          beNotEditable;
          yourself ].

    self layout replace: code with: newCode.
    code := newCode
```

As a last detail, because we love details, we do not want "Untitled window" as the window title and we want a default extent. We define the `initializeWindow:` method.

```
MyMiniBrowserPresenter >> initializeWindow: aWindowPresenter

    aWindowPresenter
      title: 'My Mini Browser';
      initialExtent: 750@650
```

Voilà! We have a new minimal version version of the System Browser with a read-only mode. When we run `MyMiniBrowser new open`, and we select a class and a method, and we press the 'Edit' button, we see the window in Figure 11-10.

11.8 About layout recalculation

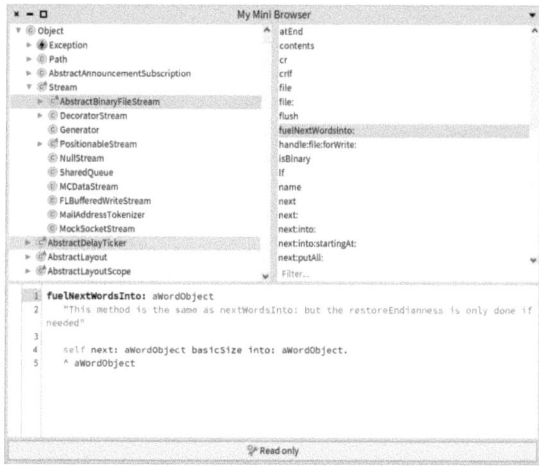

Figure 11-10 Our little browser in edit mode.

11.8 About layout recalculation

Pay attention to layout recalculation because it can have a performance penalty.

Consider a presenter having a layout with many subpresenters, and let's assume that the subpresenters have layouts with subpresenters too. Layouts allow adding and removing presenters. Those operations do not come for free. Every change to a layout triggers a recalculation because any addition or removal impacts how the presenters in the layout are displayed on the screen. So when a presenter changes multiple individual presenters of a layout, multiple recalculations may happen.

It is preferable to perform layout changes in one go. When building an initial layout, it is better to build the nested layouts bottom-up and to set the overall layout once. When updating an existing layout, it is better to build the new layout completely and set it, instead of chirurgically adding and/or removing presenters.

11.9 Conclusion

With Spec we can build applications ranging from very simple to very sophisticated. The dynamic layouts allow changing layouts on the fly. Layouts can be configured in multiple ways, so have a look at their classes and the available examples. Spec has lots of presenters that are ready to be used. Start digging into the code to see which presenters are available, and to learn their API.

CHAPTER 12

A Concrete Case: A Mail Application

We will build a small email client application that we will elaborate on and adapt in subsequent chapters. This small app brings together in real concrete ways much of what we have seen in the previous chapters. Figure 12-1 shows the target application.

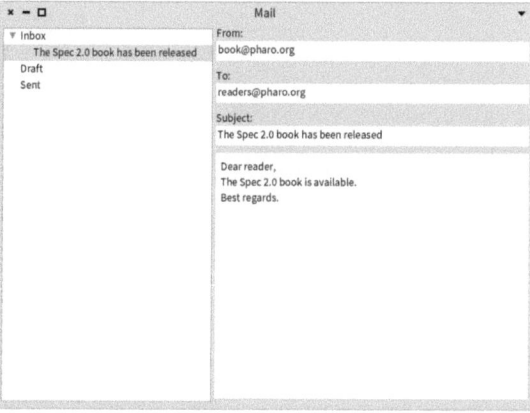

Figure 12-1   The mail client.

The example is extensive, with a lot of classes and methods. We will implement the application bottom-up. We start with the models. Afterward, we will implement the presenters that compose the application. Let's dive in.

12.1 The models

To build the mail client, we need three models (see Figure 12-2):

- `Email` represents an email.
- `MailFolder` represents a folder that holds emails, like "Inbox", "Draft", and "Sent".
- `MailAccount` represents a mail account. It holds all the emails.

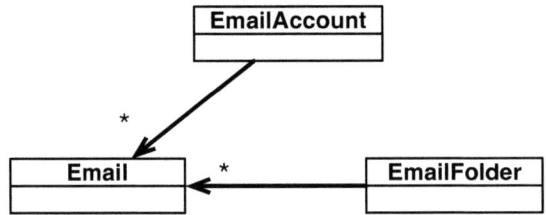

Figure 12-2 A simple model.

12.2 Email

In Figure 12-1, we see that the application shows four fields for an email. "From" holds sender. "To" holds the addressee. "Subject" holds the subject of an email. The nameless text field at the bottom-right holds the body of an email. Let's define an `Email` class to cover these fields.

```
Object << #Email
  slots: { #from . #to . #subject . #body . #status };
  package: 'CodeOfSpec20Book'
```

We do not show the accessors for `from`, `to`, `subject`, and `body`. They are trivial.

Note that there is a fifth instance variable called `status`. This instance variable will be used to keep track of the status of an email, either "received", "draft", or "sent". These statuses map onto the mail folders in the application, respectively "Inbox", "Draft", and "Sent". We define the following methods to change the status of an email. They will come in handy when we receive, create, or send emails.

12.2 Email

```
Email >> beReceived
    status := #received
```
```
Email >> beDraft
    status := #draft
```
```
Email >> beSent
    status := #sent
```

To know what the status of an email is, we define three more messages.

```
Email >> isReceived
    ^ status = #received
```
```
Email >> isDraft
    ^ status = #draft
```
```
Email >> isSent
    ^ status = #sent
```

We will not define accessors for the status instance variable. The six methods above keep the status nicely encapsulated.

Now we can define the initialize method. It states that a new email is in draft status by default.

```
Email >> initialize
    super initialize.
    self beDraft
```

We define two final methods. They are related to including emails in a tree presenter. The first method answers the string that should be displayed in the list of emails.

```
Email >> displayName
    ^ subject
```

The second method answers what should be displayed as children in a tree presenter. While a folder has children, i.e. its emails, an email does not have any children, so this method returns an empty array. We do not use tree-related terminology, as it would not be appropriate. Therefore we use content, as in "the content of a folder".

```
Email >> content

    ^ Array new
```

12.3 MailFolder

The tree on the left side of the window does not only displays emails. It also displays mail folders, which group emails according to their state. We will define the `MailFolder` model very simplisticly. It has a name and it holds emails.

```
Object << #MailFolder
   slots: { #emails . #name };
   package: 'CodeOfSpec20Book'
```

At initialization time, a `MailFolder` does not have any emails, and its name is `New folder`.

```
MailFolder >> initialize

    super initialize.
    emails := OrderedCollection new.
    name := 'New folder'
```

That defines the default state of a `MailFolder` instance, but an instance creation method is handy:

```
MailFolder class >> named: aString emails: aCollection

    ^ self new
        name: aString;
        emails: aCollection;
        yourself
```

The method above needs these accessor methods:

```
MailFolder >> emails: aCollection

    emails := aCollection
```

```
MailFolder >> name: aString

    name := aString
```

Similarly to the `Email` class, we need some tree-related methods:

```
MailFolder >> displayName

    ^ name
```

```
MailFolder >> content
    ^ emails
```

From this implementation, you can see that a `MailFolder` is just a named container object for emails, which can be used to structure the display of emails in a tree presenter.

Distinguishing emails and folders

In our target application, folders and emails are shown in a tree. A selection in the tree can be a folder or an email. If a presenter has to act differently based on the type of the selection, it needs a way to distinguish folders and emails. To keep things simple, we will introduce two methods on the model classes that we have defined so far.

```
Email >> isEmail
    ^ true
```

```
Folder >> isEmail
    ^ false
```

12.4 MailAccount

A `MailAccount` holds all emails, so the definition of the class is simple:

```
Model << #MailAccount
    slots: { #emails };
    package: 'CodeOfSpec20Book'
```

Note that this is the first email client model class that inherits from `Model`. To keep things simple, the email client application will depend only on a `MailAccount` instance, not on `Email` and `MailFolder` instances.

Initialization is trivial:

```
MailAccount >> initialize

    super initialize.
    emails := OrderedCollection new
```

We know that emails have a status and that the status is used to split emails in separate folders. That is where the following methods come in:

```
MailAccount >> receivedEmails

    ^ emails select: [ :each | each isReceived ]
```

```
MailAccount >> draftEmails

    ^ emails select: [ :each | each isDraft ]
```

```
MailAccount >> sentEmails

    ^ emails select: [ :each | each isSent ]
```

Given that `MailAccount` is the main model of the application, it defines some actions.

First of all, emails can be fetched. In a real application, emails come from a server. We do not want to go that far. Therefore, we put one email in the account.

```
MailAccount >> fetchMail

    | email |
    email := Email new
        from: 'book@pharo.org';
        to: 'readers@pharo.org';
        subject: 'The Spec 2.0 book has been released';
        body: 'Dear reader,
The Spec 2.0 book is available.
Best regards.';
        beReceived;
        yourself.
    (emails includes: email) ifFalse: [ emails add: email ].
    self changed
```

This method creates a new email, and gives it the "received" status. Then it adds the email to the emails it already holds. Adding is done conditionally because we do not want the same email appearing twice after fetching multiple times.

Note `self changed` at the end. It notifies dependents that a `MailAccount` instance changed in a general way. Again, we like to keep things simple. More specific change messages are possible, but we do not need them in this example application.

The user of the application can create new emails and save them. When they are saved, they are draft emails, as this method defines:

```
MailAccount >> saveAsDraft: anEmail

    anEmail beDraft.
    (emails includes: anEmail) ifFalse: [ emails add: anEmail ].
    self changed
```

Saving a method as draft is implemented as changing the status to "draft" and adding it to the emails, if it is not present yet. The conditional addition allows saving an email multiple times without adding it multiple times.

The method to send an email is similar to the method to save an email:

```
MailAccount >> send: anEmail

  anEmail beSent.
  (emails includes: anEmail) ifFalse: [ emails add: anEmail ].
  self changed
```

Finally, an email can be deleted. The implementation is simple. Remove the email from the account and let dependents know.

```
MailAccount >> delete: anEmail

  emails remove: anEmail.
  self changed
```

That concludes our models. Now we can dig into the presenters.

12.5 The presenters

Many presenters are composed of smaller presenters. That is also the case here. We need a presenter to display an email. We also need a presenter to display the tree of emails. When no email is selected in the tree, we like to display an informational message. That is also a presenter. And the overall application, that ties everything together, is also a presenter. So we have four presenters:

- `EmailPresenter` displays an `Email`, either editable or read-only. The fields are editable when the email is draft. The fields are read-only when the email is received or sent.

- `NoEmailPresenter` displays an informative message to tell that no email has been selected.

- `MailReaderPresenter` is responsible to show an email or the informational message. It uses the two presenters above to achieve that.

- `MailAccountPresenter` displays the tree of folders and emails.

- `MailClientPresenter` is the main presenter. It combines a `MailAccountPresenter` and a `MailReaderPresenter` to implement the email client functionality.

12.6 The `EmailPresenter`

This presenter is fairly easy. It is a view on an `Email`. Therefore it defines instance variables for all aspects of an `Email`, except the `status`.

```
SpPresenterWithModel << #EmailPresenter
  slots: { #from . #to . #subject . #body };
  package: 'CodeOfSpec20Book'
```

Note that the presenter class inherits from `SpPresenterWithModel`, which means that `model` accessors are available. An instance of `EmailPresenter` cannot function without an email, as expressed by the `initialize` method. It sets the model to an empty `Email`. Remember that a new `Email` is in draft status by default.

```
EmailPresenter >> initialize

  self model: Email new.
  super initialize
```

As always, we have to define some crucial methods.

```
EmailPresenter >> initializePresenters

  from := self newTextInput.
  to := self newTextInput.
  subject := self newTextInput.
  body := self newText
```

```
EmailPresenter >> defaultLayout

  | toLine subjectLine fromLine |
  fromLine := SpBoxLayout newTopToBottom
    add: 'From:' expand: false;
    add: from expand: false;
    yourself.
  toLine := SpBoxLayout newTopToBottom
    add: 'To:' expand: false;
    add: to expand: false;
    yourself.
  subjectLine := SpBoxLayout newTopToBottom
    add: 'Subject:' expand: false;
    add: subject expand: false;
    yourself.
  ^ SpBoxLayout newTopToBottom
      spacing: 10;
      add: fromLine expand: false;
      add: toLine expand: false;
      add: subjectLine expand: false;
```

```
        add: body;
        yourself
```

The `from`, `to`, and `subject` fields and their associated labels have their own layout. Note that `body` does not have an associated label. It is clear from the context that the field holds the body of an email. The overall layout is a vertical box layout with 10 pixels white space between the fields.

The method `connectPresenters` states that changes to fields should be stored in the email, which is held in the `model` of the `EmailPresenter`.

```
EmailPresenter >> connectPresenters

  from whenTextChangedDo: [ :text | self model from: text ].
  to whenTextChangedDo: [ :text | self model to: text ].
  subject whenTextChangedDo: [ :text | self model subject: text ].
  body whenTextChangedDo: [ :text | self model body: text ]
```

For convenience later on, we define two extra methods to make the fields editable or read-only.

```
EmailPresenter >> beEditable

  from editable: true.
  to editable: true.
  subject editable: true.
  body editable: true
```

```
EmailPresenter >> beReadOnly

  from editable: false.
  to editable: false.
  subject editable: false.
  body editable: false
```

12.7 The NoEmailPresenter

This presenter will be used when there is no selection in the tree of folders and emails. It is very simple, as it does not have any functionality.

```
SpPresenter << #NoEmailPresenter
  slots: { #message };
  package: 'CodeOfSpec20Book'
```

```
NoEmailPresenter >> initializePresenters

  message := self newLabel
    label: 'Select an email from the list to read it.';
    yourself
```

We put the message in the center of the presenter by using hAlignCenter and vAlignCenter.

```
NoEmailPresenter >> defaultLayout

  ^ SpBoxLayout newTopToBottom
    hAlignCenter;
    vAlignCenter;
    add: message;
    yourself
```

That's all there is to it.

12.8 The MailReaderPresenter

It is time to combine the two previous presenters. That is the responsibility of the MailReaderPresenter. This illustrates that we can change dynamically layouts to display different subpresenters.

```
SpPresenter << #MailReaderPresenter
  slots: { #content . #noContent };
  package: 'CodeOfSpec20Book'
```

As you can see, there are two instance variables to hold instances of the two previous presenter classes. Note that the presenter class inherits from SpPresenter, not SpPresenterWithModel, which means that a MailReaderPresenter does not have a model. We assume that instances of MailReaderPresenter will be told to update themselves.

```
MailReaderPresenter >> initializePresenters

  content := EmailPresenter new.
  noContent := NoEmailPresenter new
```

The presenter has two states. Either there is an Email, or either there isn't. We have a layout for each state. When there is an email, we will use the emailLayout:

```
MailReaderPresenter >> emailLayout

  ^ SpBoxLayout newLeftToRight
      add: content;
      yourself
```

When there is no email, we will use the noEmailLayout:

```
MailReaderPresenter >> noEmailLayout

    ^ SpBoxLayout newLeftToRight
        add: noContent;
        yourself
```

By default, we assume there is no email. After all, no method initializes the email. So the defaultLayout is the noEmailLayout.

```
MailReaderPresenter >> defaultLayout

    ^ self noEmailLayout
```

As mentioned before, we assume that instances of MailReaderPresenter will be told to update themselves. read: is the message to tell them.

```
MailReaderPresenter >> read: email

    email
        ifNil: [ self updateLayoutForNoEmail ]
        ifNotNil: [ self updateLayoutForEmail: email ]
```

The method read: delegates to the methods that do the actual work.

```
MailReaderPresenter >> updateLayoutForEmail: email

    content model: email.
    self layout: self emailLayout.
    email isDraft
        ifTrue: [ content beEditable ]
        ifFalse: [ content beReadOnly ]
```

```
MailReaderPresenter >> updateLayoutForNoEmail

    self layout: self noEmailLayout
```

These methods simply switch the layout. Note that the first one tells the EmailPresenter to be editable or read-only based on the draft status of an Email.

12.9 The MailAccountPresenter

Now we define a crucial part of the functionality of the mail client application. The MailAccountPresenter holds a tree of folders and emails.

```
SpPresenterWithModel << #MailAccountPresenter
    slots: { #foldersAndEmails };
    package: 'CodeOfSpec20Book'
```

Note that the presenter class inherits from SpPresenterWithModel because it will hold a MailAccount instance as its model, which holds the emails to show in the tree. The method initializePresenters defines the tree.

```
MailAccountPresenter >> initializePresenters

  foldersAndEmails := self newTree
    roots: Array new;
    display: [ :node | node displayName ];
    children: [ :node | node content ];
    expandRoots
```

Let's dissect the method.

- By default, the tree has no roots. Later we will set as roots the draft, inbox, and sent elements (see method modelChanged below).

- The tree presenter uses the display: block to fetch a string representation of each tree node. In the block, we send the message displayName that we defined on the model classes Email and Folder.

- The tree presenter uses the children block to fetch the children of a tree node. Folders have children, Emails do not. In the block, we send content. Remember that a Folder instance will answer its emails, and an Email instance answers an empty array, which means that emails are the leaves of the tree.

- We send the message expandRoots to expand the whole tree.

The layout is a simple box layout with the tree presenter:

```
MailAccountPresenter >> defaultLayout

  ^ SpBoxLayout newTopToBottom
      add: foldersAndEmails;
      yourself
```

By default, the tree is empty. When the model changes, the tree should be updated. Since the class MailAccountPresenter inherits from the class SpPresenterWithModel, we have the method modelChanged at our disposal.

```
MailAccountPresenter >> modelChanged

  | inbox draft sent |
  inbox := MailFolder named: 'Inbox' emails: self model receivedEmails.
  draft := MailFolder named: 'Draft' emails: self model draftEmails.
  sent := MailFolder named: 'Sent' emails: self model sentEmails.
  foldersAndEmails
    roots: { inbox . draft . sent };
    expandRoots
```

The model is a `MailAccount` instance. The method filters the emails of that instance based on their status and creates folders, each holding emails with the same status. The method sends `receivedEmails`, `draftEmails`, and `sentEmails`. The corresponding methods were defined when we defined the `MailAccount` class. The three folders become the roots of the tree, and the roots are expanded with the `expandRoots` message so that the user sees the whole tree.

When implementing a presenter with a tree, or any widget that has a selection, it is always a good idea to define a method that allows reacting to selection changes. We will need the method later to connect the `MailAccountPresenter` to the `MailReader`.

```
MailAccountPresenter >> whenSelectionChangedDo: aBlock

    foldersAndEmails whenSelectionChangedDo: aBlock
```

The method simply delegates to the tree presenter held by `foldersAndEmails`.

We define two extra methods related to selection that will come in handy later on. The first method returns a boolean that indicates whether an email is selected. We only have two levels in the tree, so if the path to the selection has two elements, we know that an email has been selected. The second method simply returns the selected item in the tree.

```
MailAccountPresenter >> hasSelectedEmail

    ^ foldersAndEmails selection selectedPath size = 2
```

```
MailAccountPresenter >> selectedItem

    ^ foldersAndEmails selectedItem
```

Apart from making selections, the `MailAccountPresenter` does not provide any functionality. Not yet. We will introduce it later when we need it.

We are almost there. One presenter to go.

12.10 The `MailClientPresenter`

This presenter combines all the presenters that we have introduced so far. We start with an initial version of the presenter class. In subsequent sections, we will elaborate on the class.

```
SpPresenterWithModel << #MailClientPresenter
    slots: { #account . #reader . #editedEmail };
    package: 'CodeOfSpec20Book'
```

The class inherits from SpPresenterWithModel. The model is a MailAccount instance. There are three instance variables. The first two hold presenters. The third holds the email that is being edited.

```
MailClientPresenter >> initializePresenters

  account := MailAccountPresenter on: self model.
  reader := MailReaderPresenter new
```

We use a paned layout, with 40% of the space allocated to the MailAccountPresenter:

```
MailClientPresenter >> defaultLayout

  ^ SpPanedLayout newLeftToRight
      positionOfSlider: 40 percent;
      add: account;
      add: reader;
      yourself
```

Let's connect the two presenters so that a selection in the tree on the left results in showing details of the selection on the right. We introduce two methods: connectPresenters and updateAfterSelectionChangedTo:

- The method connectPresenters sends the selected tree item to the reader and uses the following method.
- The method updateAfterSelectionChangedTo: to allow for post selection actions.

```
MailClientPresenter >> connectPresenters

  account whenSelectionChangedDo: [ :selection |
    | selectedFolderOrEmail |
    selectedFolderOrEmail := selection selectedItem.
    reader read: selectedFolderOrEmail.
    self updateAfterSelectionChangedTo: selectedFolderOrEmail ]
```

In the second method updateAfterSelectionChangedTo:, we use several messages that we defined earlier.

```
MailClientPresenter >> updateAfterSelectionChangedTo:
    selectedFolderOrEmail

  editedEmail := (self isDraftEmail: selectedFolderOrEmail)
    ifTrue: [ selectedFolderOrEmail ]
    ifFalse: [ nil ]
```

The method updateAfterSelectionChangedTo: keeps track of the email if it is a draft email, so that the presenter has it handy when needed. The method

12.11 First full application

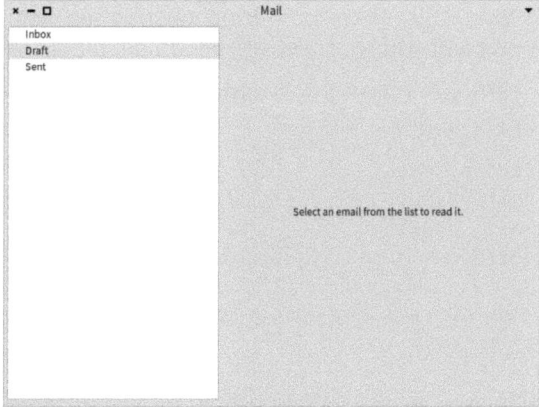

Figure 12-3 The basic mail client.

invokes the method `isDraftEmail:` (defined below) to determine whether the tree selection is a draft email.

```
^ folderOrEmailOrNil isNotNil and: [ folderOrEmailOrNil isEmail and:
    [ folderOrEmailOrNil isDraft ] ]
```

The method states that the content of the `MailReaderPresenter` held by `reader` depends on the selection in the tree. If an email is selected, the reader shows its fields. If there is no selection, or a folder is selected, the reader shows the informational message. When a draft email is selected, we put it in the `editedMail` instance variable, which will be handy when we start performing actions on the selected email.

Let's also define the method `initializeWindow`, so that the window has a title and it is big enough for reading emails easily.

```
MailClientPresenter >> initializeWindow: aWindowPresenter

    aWindowPresenter
        title: 'Mail';
        initialExtent: 650@500
```

12.11 First full application

After typing all the code, it is time to open the mail client.

```
(MailClientPresenter on: MailAccount new) open
```

Figure 12-3 shows the result. There is nothing much to see. Only three empty folders. Selecting one will still show the informational message on the right.

We can do better. Let's add a draft email with the `saveAsDraft:` message that we defined in `MailAccount`.

```
account := MailAccount new.
email := Email new subject: 'My first email'.
account saveAsDraft: email.
(MailClientPresenter on: account) open
```

That opens a window with a draft email. After selecting it, the window looks as shown in Figure 12-4.

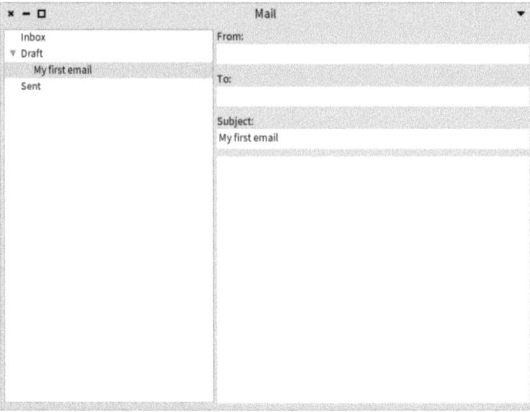

Figure 12-4 The basic mail client with a draft email.

12.12 Conclusion

This was a long chapter with an extensive example with multiple models and multiple presenters. It lays the foundation for the next chapters, where we will extend the main presenter and adapt the subpresenters to explain more Spec functionality.

CHAPTER 13

Menubar, Toolbar, Status Bar, and Context Menus

Often application windows have a menubar that includes all commands provided by the application. Application windows may also have a toolbar, with buttons for commands that are used frequently. Some applications only have a toolbar. Apart from supporting a menubar and toolbar, Spec supports a status bar at the bottom of a window. Some widgets, such as text fields, tables, and lists, are equipped with context menus. All these aspects are the subject of this chapter.

We will improve the email client application we built in Chapter 12. We will add a menubar, a toolbar, a status bar, and a context menu. Figure 13-1 shows the result that we like to achieve.

13.1 Adding a menubar to a window

With all the models and presenters in place as described in the previous chapter, we can dive into the subject of this chapter – remember that all the code is available as explained in Chapter 1. We start by adding a menubar with commands to manipulate emails.

A menubar is part of a window presenter. Therefore it is configured in the `initializeWindow:` method. A `SpWindowPresenter` instance understands the message `menu:` to set the menubar.

Menubar, Toolbar, Status Bar, and Context Menus

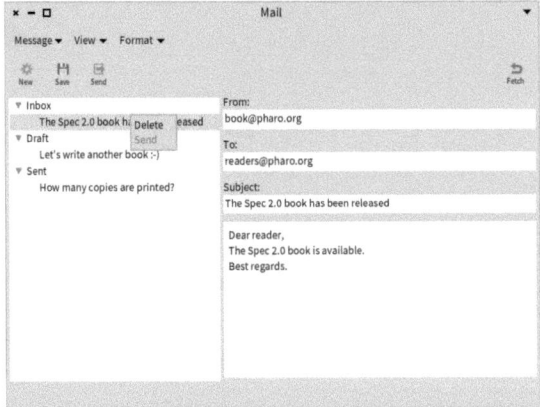

Figure 13-1 The mail client with toolbar.

```
MailClientPresenter >> initializeWindow: aWindowPresenter

    aWindowPresenter
        title: 'Mail';
        initialExtent: 650@500;
        menu: menuBar
```

The instance variable `menuBar` is not defined yet, so let's do that first. We add it to the class definition.

```
SpPresenterWithModel << #MailClientPresenter
    slots: { #account . #reader . #editedEmail . #menuBar };
    package: 'CodeOfSpec20Book'
```

Then we have to bind it. We elaborate the `initializePresenters` method to initialize the `menuBar` instance. The method delegates that responsibility to the method `initializeMenuBar`.

```
MailClientPresenter >> initializePresenters

    account := MailAccountPresenter on: self model.
    reader := MailReaderPresenter new.
    self initializeMenuBar
```

```
MailClientPresenter >> initializeMenuBar

    menuBar := self newMenuBar
        addItem: [ :item |
            item
                name: 'Message';
```

```
            subMenu: self messageMenu;
            yourself ];
        addItem: [ :item |
          item
            name: 'View';
            subMenu: self viewMenu;
            yourself ];
        addItem: [ :item |
          item
            name: 'Format';
            subMenu: self formatMenu;
            yourself ];
        yourself
```

The expression `self newMenuBar` creates a new `SpMenuBarPresenter` instance. We add three items to it. These items are the main menu items of the menubar. We configure each one with their name and their submenu.

13.2 Implementing message menu commands

In this chapter, we will implement the commands of the "Message" menu.

The two other menus, "View" and "Format" are included only to show you multiple menus in the menubar. But the method `viewMenu` and `formatMenu` are basically empty and doing nothing besides creating empty menus. We start with the menus that we will not implement. They are short.

```
MailClientPresenter >> viewMenu
  "Empty placeholder Not defined in this chapter"
  ^ self newMenu
      addItem: [ :item | item name: 'Show CC field' ];
      addItem: [ :item | item name: 'Show BCC field' ];
      yourself
```

```
MailClientPresenter >> formatMenu
  "Empty placeHolder. Not defined in this chapter"
  ^ self newMenu
      addItem: [ :item | item name: 'Plain text' ];
      addItem: [ :item | item name: 'Rich text' ];
      yourself
```

Now we are ready to focus on the "Message" menu commands. We will implement all commands of the "Message" menu. That requires some code:

```
MailClientPresenter >> messageMenu

  ^ self newMenu
      addGroup: [ :group |
```

```
      group
        addItem: [ :item |
          item
            name: 'New';
            shortcut: $n meta;
            action: [ self newMail ] ];
        addItem: [ :item |
          item
            name: 'Save';
            shortcut: $s meta;
            enabled: [ self hasDraft ];
            action: [ self saveMail ] ];
        addItem: [ :item |
          item
            name: 'Delete';
            shortcut: $d meta;
            enabled: [ self hasSelectedEmail ];
            action: [ self deleteMail ] ];
        addItem: [ :item |
          item
            name: 'Send';
            shortcut: $l meta;
            enabled: [ self hasDraft ];
            action: [ self sendMail ] ] ];
  addGroup: [ :group |
    group
      addItem: [ :item |
        item
          name: 'Fetch';
          shortcut: $f meta;
          action: [ self fetchMail ] ];
    yourself ]
```

While the first two menus included two commands, this menu includes several commands in two groups. With the `addGroup` message, we add the groups and we nest the menu items in the groups by sending the message `addItem:` to the groups. As you can see, the menu items have a name, a keyboard shortcut, and an action block. A few items have a block that defines whether they are enabled. The block argument of the `enabled:` message is evaluated each time the menu item is displayed, so that the menu item can be enabled or disabled dynamically. Note that block arguments of the `enabled:` messages send the messages `hasDraft` and `hasSelectedEmail`. We did not define the corresponding methods yet, so let's do that now. The implementations are straightforward.

```
MailClientPresenter >> hasDraft

  ^ editedEmail isNotNil
```

```
MailClientPresenter >> hasSelectedEmail

    ^ account hasSelectedEmail
```

Look at the shortcuts in the `messageMenu` method. `$n meta` means that the character "n" can be pressed together with the meta key (Command on macOS, Control on Windows and Linux) to trigger the command.

13.3 Installing shortcuts

Adding shortcuts to menu items does not automatically install them. Keyboard shortcuts have to be installed after the window has been opened. Therefore we have to adapt the `initializeWindow:` method with the `whenOpenedDo:` message, so that the keyboard shortcuts can be installed after opening the window. `SpMenuPresenter`, which is the superclass of `SpMenuBarPresenter`, implements the method `addKeybindingsTo:`, which comes in handy here.

```
MailClientPresenter >> initializeWindow: aWindowPresenter

    aWindowPresenter
        title: 'Mail';
        initialExtent: 650@500;
        menu: menuBar.
    menuBar addKeybindingsTo: aWindowPresenter
```

13.4 Defining actions

We keep the action blocks simple by sending a message. We have to implement them of course, so let's do that. Based on the models that we defined earlier in this chapter, the implementation of the actions is fairly straightforward.

```
MailClientPresenter >> newMail

    editedEmail := Email new.
    editedEmail beDraft.
    reader updateLayoutForEmail: editedEmail.
    self modelChanged
```

```
MailClientPresenter >> saveMail

    account saveAsDraft: editedEmail.
    editedEmail := nil.
    self modelChanged
```

```
MailClientPresenter >> deleteMail

    account deleteMail.
    self modelChanged

MailClientPresenter >> sendMail

    account sendMail: editedEmail.
    editedEmail := nil.
    self modelChanged

MailClientPresenter >> fetchMail

    account fetchMail.
    self modelChanged
```

It is time to try it out. To see the menubar in action, let's open a window with:

```
(MailClientPresenter on: MailAccount new) open
```

Figure 13-2 shows the window. The menubar includes the three menus we defined. The figure shows the open "Message" menu. It has two groups of menu items, separated by a horizontal line. Two menu items are enabled. Three menu items are disabled because they are actions on an email but no email is selected.

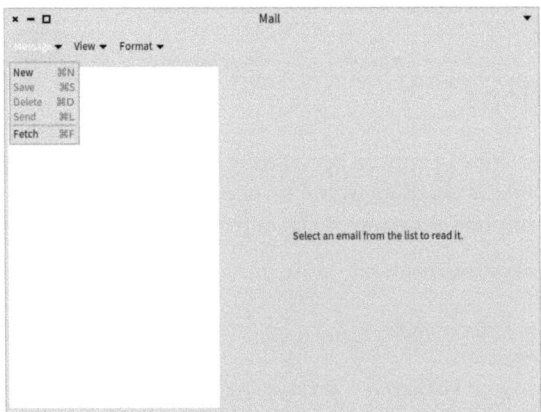

Figure 13-2   The mail client with a menu opened from the menubar.

13.5 Adding a toolbar to a window

Some actions are so common that it is useful to have them one click away. That is where the toolbar comes in. A toolbar allows putting actions as buttons in the user interface (See Figure 13-3).

Not surprisingly, like the menubar, the toolbar is part of a window presenter. So we have to revisit the `initializeWindow:` method. A SpWindowPresenter instance understands the message `toolbar:` to set the toolbar.

```
MailClientPresenter >> initializeWindow: aWindowPresenter

    aWindowPresenter
        title: 'Mail';
        initialExtent: 650@500;
        menu: menuBar;
        toolbar: toolBar.
        menuBar addKeybindingsTo: aWindowPresenter
```

`toolbar` is an instance variable, so we have to elaborate the class definition:

```
SpPresenterWithModel << #MailClientPresenter
    slots: { #account . #reader . #editedEmail . #menuBar . #toolBar };
    package: 'CodeOfSpec20Book'
```

Similar to what we did for the menubar, we define a method `initializeToolBar` and use it in `initializePresenters`.

```
MailClientPresenter >> initializePresenters

    account := MailAccountPresenter on: self model.
    reader := MailReaderPresenter new.
    self initializeMenuBar.
    self initializeToolBar
```

```
MailClientPresenter >> initializeToolBar

    | newButton fetchButton |
    newButton := self newToolbarButton
        label: 'New';
        icon: (self iconNamed: #smallNew);
        help: 'New email';
        action: [ self newMail ];
        yourself.
    saveButton := self newToolbarButton
        label: 'Save';
        icon: (self iconNamed: #smallSave);
        help: 'Save email';
        action: [ self saveMail ];
        yourself.
```

```
sendButton := self newToolbarButton
    label: 'Send';
    icon: (self iconNamed: #smallExport);
    help: 'Send email';
    action: [ self sendMail ];
    yourself.
fetchButton := self newToolbarButton
    label: 'Fetch';
    icon: (self iconNamed: #refresh);
    help: 'Fetch emails from server';
    action: [ self fetchMail ];
    yourself.
toolBar := self newToolbar
    addItem: newButton;
    addItem: saveButton;
    addItem: sendButton;
    addItemRight: fetchButton;
    yourself
```

This method defines four buttons, of which two are held in instance variables. Shortly, it will become clear why. Of course, we have to adapt the class definition again:

```
SpPresenterWithModel << #MailClientPresenter
    slots: { #account . #reader . #editedEmail . #menuBar . #toolBar .
        #sendButton . #saveButton };
    package: 'CodeOfSpec20Book'
```

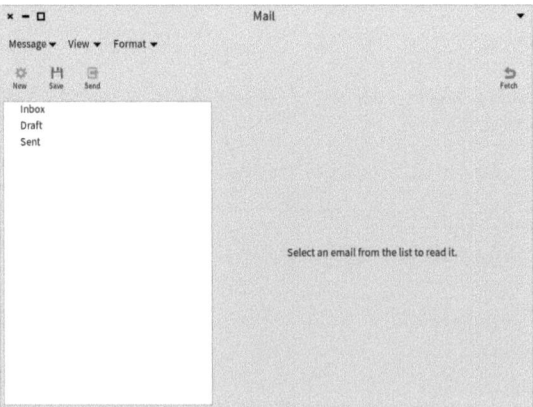

Figure 13-3 The mail client with disabled buttons in a toolbar.

The `initializeToolBar` method adds four buttons to the toolbar. A toolbar has two sections, one on the left and one on the right. With the message addItem: we add the first three buttons to the left section. With the message addItemRight: we add one button to the right section.

Each button has a label, an icon, a help text, and an action. As we did in initializeMenuBar, we use simple action blocks that send a message to the mail client presenter. These are the same messages that we used in the action blocks of the menu items in the "Message" menu in the menubar. That means that we are done.

13.6 Supporting enablement

We said we were done but well, not really. The menu items had a block to determine whether they were enabled or disabled. That is not the case for toolbar buttons, because they are visible all the time. Therefore we have to manage enablement of the buttons explicitly. Every time the state of the mail client changes, we have to update the enablement of the toolbar buttons. We introduce a new method updateToolBarButtons to do that. Based on messages that were defined before, we can set the enablement state of the saveButton and the sendButton. That is why we defined both as instance variables. The two other buttons are always enabled, so it is not needed to hold them in instance variables.

```
MailClientPresenter >> updateToolBarButtons

    | hasSelectedDraft |
    hasSelectedDraft := self hasDraft.
    saveButton enabled: hasSelectedDraft.
    sendButton enabled: hasSelectedDraft
```

To finish the toolbar functionality, we have to send updateToolBarButtons in the appropriate places. Everywhere the state of the mail client presenter changes, we have to send the message. You may think we have to do that in many places, but we have implemented the presenter class in such a way that there are only two places where it is required.

First, MailClientPresenter inherits from SpPresenterWithModel, which means that every time the model of an instance changes, it sends modelChanged. So we can update the toolbar buttons in that method.

```
MailClientPresenter >> modelChanged

    self updateToolBarButtons
```

Second, we have to set the initial state of the toolbar buttons when the mail client presenter is initialized. The method updateAfterSelectionChangedTo:, invoked by the method connectPresenters, is a good place to update the toolbar buttons. We add an extra line at the bottom of the method that we defined before.

```
MailClientPresenter >> updateAfterSelectionChangedTo:
    selectedFolderOrEmail

    super updateAfterSelectionChangedTo: selectedFolderOrEmail.
    self updateToolBarButtons
```

As for the menubar, it required a lot of code to setup the toolbar and wire everything, but we are ready. Let's open the window again.

```
(MailClientPresenter on: MailAccount new) open
```

Figure 13-3 shows the window. It has a menubar and a toolbar. Three toolbar buttons are placed on the left side, and one button is placed at the right side. That corresponds to our configuration of the toolbar. The save button and the send button are greyed out because they are disabled.

Let's create a new email by pressing the toolbar button labeled "New" and see how the enablement state of the toolbar buttons changes. Figure 13-4 shows that all the buttons are enabled.

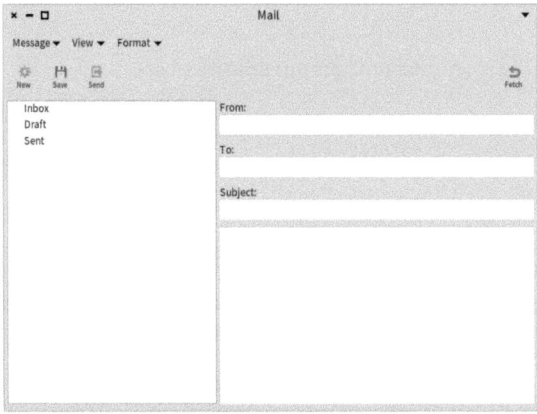

Figure 13-4 The mail client with enabled buttons in a toolbar.

13.7 Adding a status bar to a window

After adding a menubar and a toolbar, we will add a status bar (see Figures 13-5 and 13-6). A status bar is useful to show short messages for some time, or until the next message appears. We will elaborate the mail client presenter to show messages to inform the user that actions have been performed.

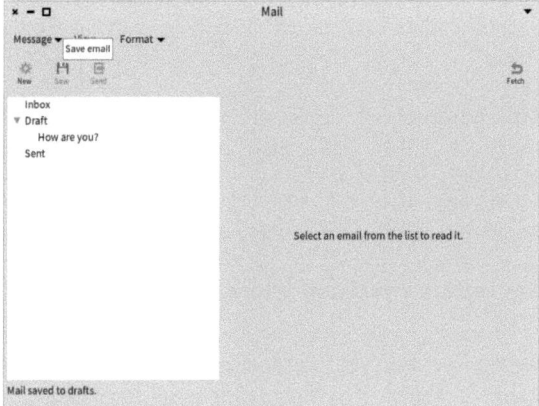

Figure 13-5 The email has been saved.

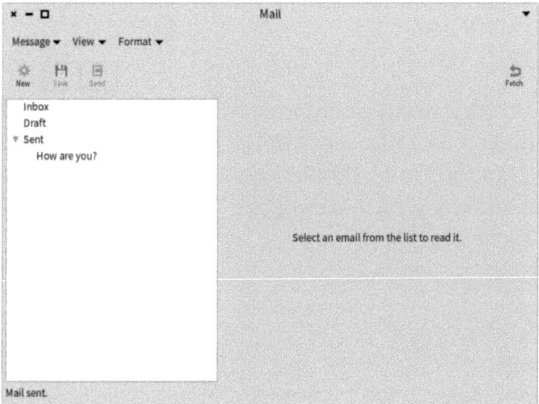

Figure 13-6 The email has been sent.

The status bar appears at the bottom of the window. As with the menubar and the toolbar, we add it in the method initializeWindow:.

```
MailClientPresenter >> initializeWindow: aWindowPresenter

    aWindowPresenter
        title: 'Mail';
        initialExtent: 650@500;
        menu: menuBar;
        toolbar: toolBar;
        statusBar: statusBar.
        menuBar addKeybindingsTo: aWindowPresenter
```

statusBar is a new instance variable, which we add to the class definition of the presenter.

```
SpPresenterWithModel << #MailClientPresenter
    slots: { #account . #reader . #editedEmail . #menuBar . #toolBar .
        #statusBar };
    package: 'CodeOfSpec20Book'
```

As already done twice, we adapt the initializePresenters method. The message newStatusBar creates a new SpStatusBarPresenter instance.

```
MailClientPresenter >> initializePresenters

    account := MailAccountPresenter on: self model.
    reader := MailReaderPresenter new.
    self initializeMenuBar.
    self initializeToolBar.
    statusBar := self newStatusBar
```

The status bar is no more than a container for a text message. We will adapt some action methods to put messages in the status bar. A SpStatusBarPresenter instance responds to pushMessage: and popMessage:. Let's start with the method fetchMail. We push a message "Mail fetched." to indicate that the fetch action was successful.

```
MailClientPresenter >> fetchMail

    account fetchMail.
    self modelChanged.
    statusBar pushMessage: 'Mail fetched.'
```

Then we adapt the other action methods as well.

```
MailClientPresenter >> saveMail

    account saveAsDraft: editedEmail.
    editedEmail := nil.
```

13.7 Adding a status bar to a window

```
self modelChanged.
statusBar pushMessage: 'Mail saved to drafts.'
```

```
MailClientPresenter >> sendMail

    account sendMail: editedEmail.
    editedEmail := nil.
    self modelChanged.
    statusBar pushMessage: 'Mail sent.'
```

```
MailClientPresenter >> deleteMail

    account deleteMail.
    self modelChanged.
    statusBar pushMessage: 'Mail deleted.'
```

To finish the status bar functionality, we start with a clean status bar. Therefore we adapt the method updateAfterSelectionChangedTo: again, in which we already bring the toolbar buttons in their initial enablement state. We send the message popMessage to ensure that the status bar is empty.

```
MailClientPresenter >> updateAfterSelectionChangedTo:
    selectedFolderOrEmail

    super updateAfterSelectionChangedTo: selectedFolderOrEmail.
    self updateToolBarButtons.
    statusBar popMessage
```

Let's test the mail client presenter by opening it again.

```
(MailClientPresenter on: MailAccount new) open
```

We will test a full scenario.

- After opening the window, press the "New" button and fill in the fields of the new email. Figure 13-7 shows the initial state before we start manipulating the email.

- When the fields are filled in, we save the email by pressing the save button. See Figure 13-5. The status bar shows "Mail saved to drafts." and we see the subject of the email nested under the "Draft" folder in the list on the left.

- After selecting the email in the list and pressing the "Send" button, we see the situation in Figure 13-6. The email has moved from the "Draft" folder to the "Sent" folder, and the status bar shows "Mail sent.".

- After pressing the "Fetch" button, the fetched email appears under the "Inbox" folder in the list. The status bar shows "Mail fetched.". See Figure 13-8.

177

Menubar, Toolbar, Status Bar, and Context Menus

- After selecting the email in the "Inbox" and choosing "Delete" from the "Message" menu, the email is removed from the list, and the status bar shows "Mail deleted.". See Figure 13-9.

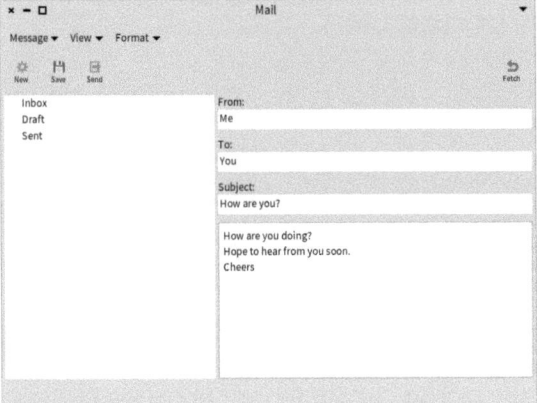

Figure 13-7   A new email.

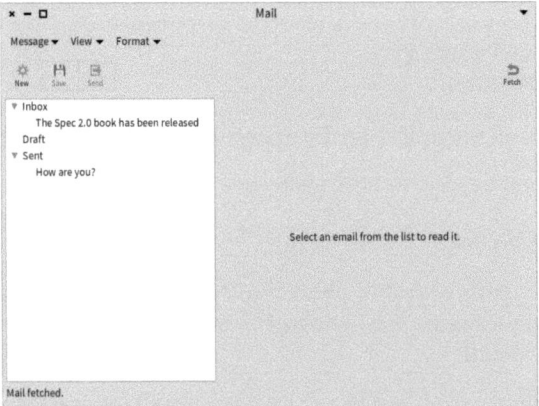

Figure 13-8   Email has been fetched.

All actions that change the status bar have been tested.

13.8 Adding a context menu to a presenter

The final step to complete the mail client presenter is the addition of a context menu. We will add a context menu to the tree with the folders and emails. We

13.8 Adding a context menu to a presenter

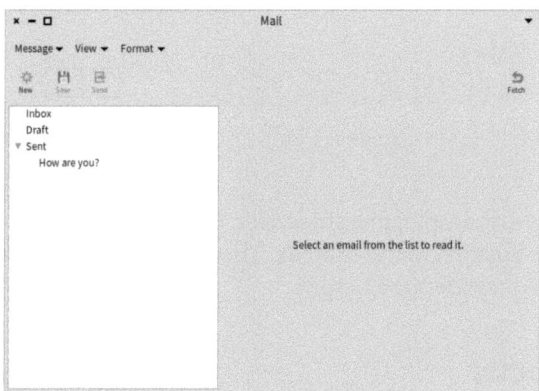

Figure 13-9 The email has been deleted.

will not add a big context menu. For demonstration purposes, we will restrict the menu to two menu items, one to delete an email and one to send an email.

The tree includes folders and emails, so the desired menu items should be disabled when a folder is selected. They should also be disabled when no selection has been made. On top of that condition, the send command can only be applied to emails that are in the "Draft" folder because received and sent mails cannot be sent.

Typically, a presenter adds a context menu to a subpresenter. Given that the tree of folders and emails is a subpresenter of the MailAccountPresenter, we would expect the MailAccountPresenter to install a context menu on the tree presenter. However, the MailAccountPresenter cannot decide what needs to be done for deleting or sending an email. What needs to be done is the responsibility of the MailClientPresenter, which defines the methods deleteMail and sendMail. Both methods do what they have to do to perform the action, and then send the modelChanged message and update the status bar.

Therefore MailClientPresenter defines the menu.

```
MailClientPresenter >> accountMenu

    ^ self newMenu
        addItem: [ :item |
            item
                name: 'Delete';
                enabled: [ self hasSelectedEmail ];
                action: [ self deleteMail ] ];
        addItem: [ :item |
```

```
        item
          name: 'Send';
          enabled: [ self hasSelectedEmail
                    and: [ account selectedItem isDraft] ];
          action: [ self sendMail ] ];
    yourself
```

The action blocks are simple, like the action blocks of the menu items in the menubar and the buttons in the toolbar. They send the action messages `deleteMail` and `sendMail` we have defined before.

13.9 Enabling blocks

More interestingly are the `enabled:` blocks, which define the enablement of the menu items. Deleting an email is possible only when an email is selected. That is expressed by the `enabled:` block of the "Delete" menu item. As described in the introduction of this section, sending an email is possible only if the selected email is a draft email. That is exactly what the `enabled:` block for the "Send" menu item expresses.

Note the name of the method. We use the name `accountMennu` because the context menu will be installed on the `MailAccountPresenter`. However, the context menu has to be installed on the tree presenter with the folders and the emails. Therefore `MailAccountPresenter` delegates to the tree presenter. Let's realise that in code. First, from within `initializePresenters` of `MailClientPresenter`, we send the `contextMenu:` message to install the context menu on the `MailAccountPresenter`.

```
MailClientPresenter >> initializePresenters

    account := MailAccountPresenter on: self model.
    account contextMenu: [ self accountMenu ].
    reader := MailReaderPresenter new.
    self initializeMenuBar.
    self initializeToolBar.
    statusBar := self newStatusBar
```

Then we implement the `contextMenu:` on `MailAccountPresenter`. It delegates to the tree presenter,

```
MailAccountPresenter >> contextMenu: aBlock

    foldersAndEmails contextMenu: aBlock
```

That concludes the implementation. It is time to open the window again and try the new context menu.

```
[ (MailClientPresenter on: MailAccount new) open
```

13.9 Enabling blocks

When clicking the right-button mouse button, the context menu appears. Figure 13-10 shows that the two menu items are disabled when a folder is selected

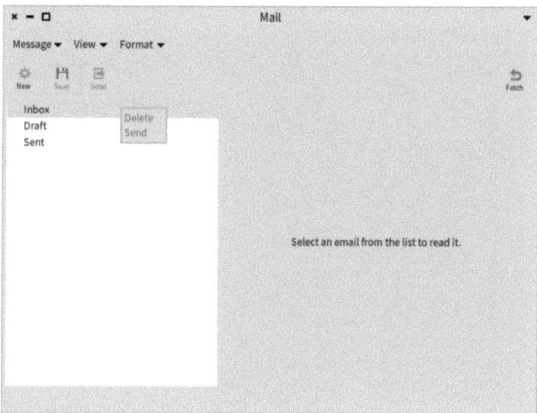

Figure 13-10 Context menu items are disabled.

After fetching email and selecting the received email, the menu includes an enabled "Delete" menu item and a disabled "Send" menu item, as shown in Figure 13-11.

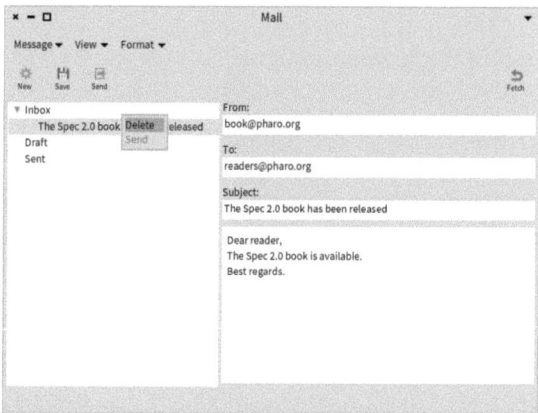

Figure 13-11 Sending a received email is not allowed.

As a final test, we create a new email, save it, and select it. It is a draft email, so it can be sent. That is what we see in the context menu in Figure 13-12. Both menu items are enabled.

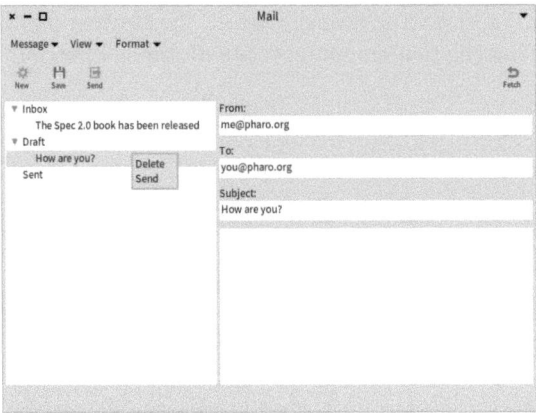

Figure 13-12 Sending a draft email is allowed.

13.10 Conclusion

We have described how to add a menubar and a toolbar to a window. It required quite some code to define the menu items and the toolbar buttons. We have also described how messages can be shown in the status bar at the bottom of a window. At the end, we also described how to add a context menu to a tree presenter.

An important aspect of menu items and toolbar buttons is their enablement based on the state of the presenter in a window. We have shown how to apply enablement, and we illustrated the behavior in several figures.

CHAPTER 14

Using transmissions and ports

This chapter introduces transmissions, which are a more compact way to connect presenters than events as shown in earlier chapters. With some examples, the different aspects of transmissions will be explained.

14.1 What are transmissions?

Transmissions are a uniform way to connect presenters, thinking about the "flow" of data more than the way data is displayed.

Each presenter defines **output ports**, which are ports to send data, and **input ports**, which are ports to receive data.

When no interaction with a presenter is possible, it will not have an output port (SpLabelPresenter for example). Some presenters have no input port (SpMenuPresenter for example). Unless you define output ports and input ports for your presenters, they do not have any ports.

When a presenter has output and input ports, it defines which ports are the default output port and the default input port.

There are different classes of ports. If you do not find a suitable port class for your presenters, you can define your own.

A transmission connects a presenter's output port with another presenter's input port. When using transmissions, instead of thinking about events and how to act on them, you think about how data flows from one presenter's output port to another presenter's input port. The event handling is taken care of by the output ports.

14.2 A simple example

Let's take a look at a very simple example. Consider a presenter that shows an overview–detail relationship. We define a class `OverviewDetailPresenter` with two instance variables to hold a `SpListPresenter` and a `SpTextPresenter`.

```
SpPresenter << #OverviewDetailPresenter
    slots: { #overview . #detail };
    package: 'CodeOfSpec20Book'
```

We populate the list with some `Point` instances.

```
OverviewDetailPresenter >> initializePresenters

    overview := self newList
        items: { 1@1 . 7@5 . 10@15 . 12@0 . 0@ -9 . -5@ -5 };
        yourself.
    detail := self newText
```

The `defaultLayout` method is straightforward. It defines a horizontal box layout.

```
OverviewDetailPresenter >> defaultLayout

    ^ SpBoxLayout newLeftToRight
        add: overview expand: false;
        add: detail;
        yourself
```

Figure 14-1 A very simple overview–detail presenter.

Here comes the most interesting method. The method `connectPresenters` connects the list to the text. We start simple with a logic that uses events and not transmissions. When a point is selected in the list, we simply show it in the text.

```
OverviewDetailPresenter >> connectPresenters

  overview whenSelectedItemChangedDo: [ :selectedPoint |
    detail text: selectedPoint asString ]
```

When we open the presenter with the snippet below, the window looks like the one shown in Figure 14-1.

```
[ OverviewDetailPresenter new open
```

14.3 Basic transmission

The method `connectPresenters` above uses the traditional way of connecting presenters. Let's use a transmission instead.

```
OverviewDetailPresenter >> connectPresenters

  overview transmitTo: detail
```

The method `transmitTo:` is the most basic way to set up a transmission. It is implemented as follows:

```
SpAbstractPresenter >> transmitTo: aPresenter

  ^ self defaultOutputPort transmitTo: aPresenter defaultInputPort
```

In our example, the method above connects the list presenter's default output port with the detail presenter's default input port. `SpAbstractPresenter >> defaultOutputPort` and `SpAbstractPresenter >> defaultInputPort` define that any presenter can have a default output and a default input port. Browse the implementors of the two methods to learn how different presenter classes use output and input ports.

Presenters can have multiple output and input ports. They can be connected by sending the message `transmitTo:` to an output port, similar to what `SpAbstractPresenter >> transmitTo:` does with the default output and input ports.

When we open the presenter again, and we select a point in the list, an exception is raised. That is because the `Point` instance transmitted from the list presenter's default output port is not compatible with the kind of object expected by the text presenter's default input port. The latter expects a `String`, not a `Point`. This is a common situation. Only in simple use cases will the transmitted object be adequate for the input port. In many cases, the transmitted object needs to be transformed to transmit an adequate object to the input port. That is where transformations come in.

14.4 Transforming a transmitted object

The object transmitted from a presenter's output port can be inadequate for the input port of another presenter. There are two reasons why a transmitted object may be inadequate:

- The kind of object coming from an output port may not be acceptable for an input port. In our simple example, that is the case. The input port expects a String, not a Point.
- The object itself coming from an output port may not be what you like to send to the input port.

Let's give examples of both reasons.

To fix the exception raised when selecting a point in the list, we adapt the method connectPresenters to answer a String instead of a Point:

```
OverviewDetailPresenter >> connectPresenters

  overview
    transmitTo: detail
    transform: [ :selectedPoint | selectedPoint asString ]
```

Now the behavior of the presenter is error-free.

Suppose that we do not like to merely show the selected point in the text, but that we like to show the distance of the selected point to the origin of the coordinate system. In the traditional way, the method connectPresenters would look like this:

```
OverviewDetailPresenter >> connectPresenters

  overview whenSelectedItemChangedDo: [ :selectedPoint |
    | distanceToOrigin |
    distanceToOrigin := selectedPoint
      ifNil: [ '' ]
      ifNotNil: [ (selectedPoint distanceTo: 0@0) asString ].
    detail text: distanceToOrigin ]
```

When using a transmission, it is reduced to:

```
OverviewDetailPresenter >> connectPresenters

  overview
    transmitTo: detail
    transform: [ :selectedPoint |
```

```
        selectedPoint
          ifNil: [ '' ]
          ifNotNil: [ (selectedPoint distanceTo: 0@0) asString ] ]
```

After opening, we see the window as shown in Figure 14-2.

Figure 14-2 The overview–detail presenter with a transformation.

14.5 Acting on a transmission without input port

Sometimes it is not necessary to send a transmitted object to the input port of a subpresenter. If your presenter has to do something when an object is being transmitted through an output port, it can use the message `transmitDo:`. The message takes a block that will be evaluated when there is a transmission.

Let's extend the simple example to show that. Suppose that for debugging purposes, we like to log the selected point to the `Transcript`. In the traditional way, we would implement `connectPresenters` like this:

```
OverviewDetailPresenter >> connectPresenters

  overview whenSelectedItemChangedDo: [ :selectedPoint |
    | distanceToOrigin |
    distanceToOrigin := selectedPoint
      ifNil: [ '' ]
      ifNotNil: [ (selectedPoint distanceTo: 0@0) asString ].
    detail text: distanceToOrigin.
    selectedPoint crTrace ]
```

With transmissions, we can achieve the same behavior as follows:

```
OverviewDetailPresenter >> connectPresenters

    overview
        transmitTo: detail
        transform: [ :selectedPoint |
            selectedPoint
                ifNil: [ '' ]
                ifNotNil: [ (selectedPoint distanceTo: 0@0) asString ] ].
    overview transmitDo: [ :selectedPoint | selectedPoint crTrace ]
```

14.6 Acting after a transmission

Sometimes, after a transmission happens, a presenter needs to modify something given the new status of a subpresenter. Examples are preselecting something, and updating the state of toolbar buttons. That is where post transmission actions come in. The messages that we have seen so far, have variations with an extra keyword argument `postTransmission:`.

Let's elaborate the simple example for the last time. Suppose we like to select the text after it has been set. In the traditional way, in the method `connectPresenters`, we would send `selectAll` to the text presenter:

```
OverviewDetailPresenter >> connectPresenters

    overview whenSelectedItemChangedDo: [ :selectedPoint |
        | distanceToOrigin |
        distanceToOrigin := selectedPoint
            ifNil: [ '' ]
            ifNotNil: [ (selectedPoint distanceTo: 0@0) asString ].
        detail text: distanceToOrigin.
        detail selectAll.
        selectedPoint crTrace ]
```

With transmissions, we would add an extra `postTransmission:` keyword to the message that we used before. The extra argument is a block that takes up to three arguments. The first argument, often called `destination`, is the presenter of the input port. The second argument, often called `origin`, is the presenter of the output port. The third argument is the transmitted object, without transformation applied to it. In our example, we only need access to the destination argument. That is why there is only one argument in the `postTransmission:` block.

```
OverviewDetailPresenter >> connectPresenters

    overview
        transmitTo: detail
        transform: [ :selectedPoint |
```

```
            selectedPoint
                ifNil: [ '' ]
                ifNotNil: [ (selectedPoint distanceTo: 0@0) asString ] ]
    postTransmission: [ :destination | destination selectAll ].
    overview transmitDo: [ :selectedPoint | selectedPoint crTrace ]
```

Let's open the presenter again to test the presenter with the transmissions.

```
OverviewDetailPresenter new open
```

After selecting a point, we see the window as shown in Figure 14-3. The distance to the origin of the coordinate system is selected in the text, and the selected point is logged in the transcript.

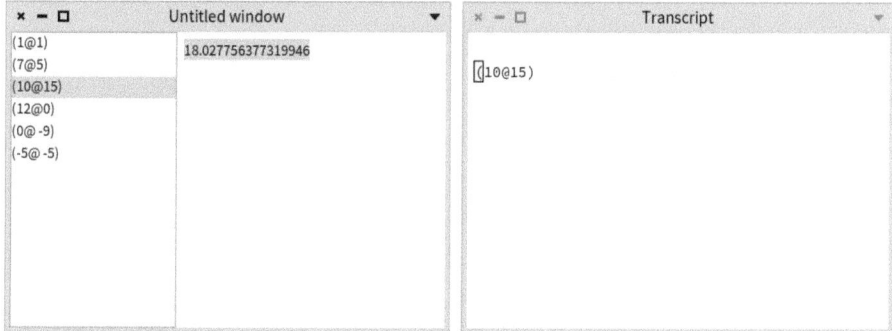

Figure 14-3 The final overview–detail presenter.

14.7 Available ports

We described a very simple, albeit often used, use case with two kinds of ports where a selected object is input for some presenter. The output port of a SpList-Presenter is an instance of SpSelectionPort. The input port of a SpTextP-resenter is a SpTextPort instance. Instances of SpSelectionPort are applicable for the output ports of presenters that implement a selection mechanism. Instances of SpTextPort are applicable for the input ports of presenters that display or edit text (see the SpAbstractTextPresenter class hierarchy). All the presenter classes that implement widgets have their particular output port and input port classes. That is why there are different classes of ports. Their common superclass is SpAbstractPort, with two direct subclasses SpInput-Port and SpOutputPort.

14.8 Ports and nesting presenters

When you implement your own presenters, they will use subpresenters that can be connected with transmissions. But what happens when you reuse your presenters in other presenters? The answer is simple: you will also use transmissions to connect them.

To make your presenters suitable for use with transmissions, the presenter classes have to define the output and input ports, and they have to implement the methods `defaultOutputPort` and `defaultInputPort`. Depending on the behavior of a presenter, the presenter class implements one or both methods. When defining the ports, you can use one of the available port classes. If you do not find a suitable port class for your presenters, you can define your own.

In some cases, it is not necessary to define new ports. Instead, delegation can be used to reuse a port of a subpresenter. We will see an example of delegation in the next section.

14.9 A more advanced example

In this section, we revisit the small email client application from Chapter 12.

Let's start with the presenter class `MailClientPresenter`. It had this method:

```
MailClientPresenter >> connectPresenters

  account whenSelectionChangedDo: [ :selection |
    | selectedFolderOrEmail |
    selectedFolderOrEmail := selection selectedItem.
    reader read: selectedFolderOrEmail.
    self updateAfterSelectionChangedTo: selectedFolderOrEmail ]
```

We adapt it to use a transmission:

```
MailClientPresenter >> connectPresenters

  account
    transmitTo: reader
    postTransmission: [ :destination :origin :selectedFolderOrEmail |
      self updateAfterSelectionChangedTo: selectedFolderOrEmail ]
```

We send the message `transmitTo:postTransmission:` to express that the selection made in the `account` presenter (an instance of `MailAccountPresenter`) should be transmitted to the `reader` presenter (an instance of `MailReaderPresenter`), and that there is a post transmission action.

Although the method `connectPresenters` expresses the desired transmission behavior very succinctly, it does not work without additional changes. After all, we did not yet define the output port of the account presenter and the input port of the reader presenter.

For the account presenter, we can simply delegate defaultOutputPort, because the default output port of the SpTreePresenter that holds the folders and the emails, is a SpSelectionPort. It will provide the selected folder or email.

```
MailAccountPresenter >> defaultOutputPort

    ^ foldersAndEmails defaultOutputPort
```

The definition of the input port of the reader presenter is a bit more complex. A MailReaderPresenter instance expects to receive a Folder or an Email instance. That is what was expressed by reader read: selectedFolderOrEmail in the original implementation of MailClientPresenter >> connectPresenters. The folder or email is in fact the model of a MailReaderPresenter, but we did not provide it by sending setModel:, but by sending read:. We used read: because conceptually it made sense in the context of a MailReaderPresenter.

There is no input port class that knows the read: protocol, so we have two options. Either we implement a new input port class, or either we use SpModelPort. We choose the latter because we prefer reusing existing classes. But that means that we will have to implement setModel: on the MailReaderPresenter class because SpModelPort sends setModel: to give the transmitted object to the destination presenter. We can simply delegate to read: to make the presenter compatible with the protocol expected by SpModelPort.

```
MailReaderPresenter >> defaultInputPort

    ^ SpModelPort newPresenter: self
```

```
MailReaderPresenter >> setModel: email

    self read: email
```

That concludes the changes to introduce a transmission at the level of the MailClientPresenter. When opening the mail client with (MailClientPresenter on: MailAccount new) open, the mail application behaves as before, but now it uses a transmission.

14.10 Another variation

There is another presenter where we can use transmissions: the EmailPresenter. Its original connectPresenters method was implemented as follows.

Using transmissions and ports

```
EmailPresenter >> connectPresenters

    from whenTextChangedDo: [ :text | self model from: text ].
    to whenTextChangedDo: [ :text | self model to: text ].
    subject whenTextChangedDo: [ :text | self model subject: text ].
    body whenTextChangedDo: [ :text | self model body: text ]
```

Although the change to use transmissions is superficial, the same behavior can be achieved with:

```
EmailPresenter >> connectPresenters

    from transmitDo: [ :text | self model from: text ].
    to transmitDo: [ :text | self model to: text ].
    subject transmitDo: [ :text | self model subject: text ].
    body transmitDo: [ :text | self model body: text ]
```

The messages `transmitDo:` is used because we like a side effect on the model. No input ports are involved in the transmissions.

14.11 Conclusion

This chapter introduced transmissions and ports, and illustrated the concepts with two examples.

Output ports define the origins of data, and the transformations to apply to the data before transmitting it to an input port. Input ports define destinations of data. Transmissions connect output ports with input ports to define the flow of data between presenters.

CHAPTER 15

Styling applications

In this chapter, we describe how to declare and use styles in Spec applications.

First, we present stylesheets and styles and then we apply styles to the Mail Application we introduced in Chapter 12. We will illustrate how Spec manages styles and how you can adapt the look of a presenter.

There are two ways to express stylesheets: one for Morphic expressed using an extended version of STON, and CSS for GTK. In this chapter, we focus on the Morphic stylesheets for Pharo 12. We give some basis before showing how to effectively use styles to enhance the look and feel of an application.

15.1 In a nutshell

An application stylesheet

In Spec, an application has a stylesheet that can be set using the message `styleSheet:`. Each application can then refine its stylesheet.

```
app styleSheet: styleSheet.
```

Declaring styles

For the Morphic backend (as opposed to the GTK one), a stylesheet is defined as a special version of a STON string that is parsed and turned into style elements. The following snippet creates a stylesheet where all the fonts are bold, and three drawing styles `red`, `bgGray`, and `blue` are defined.

Styling applications

```
(SpStyleVariableSTONReader fromString:
  '.application [
    Font { #bold: true },
    .red [ Draw { #color: #red } ],
    .bgGray [ Draw { #backgroundColor: #E2E2E2 } ],
    .blue [ Draw { #color: #blue } ]
  ]')
```

Applying styles

Each presenter can apply a stylesheet using the messages `addStyle:` and `removeStyle:`. The following example changes the color of the text of a label presenter by applying the red style.

```
label := presenter newLabel.
label label: 'I am a label'.
label addStyle: 'red'
```

15.2 How do styles work?

Styles in Spec work like CSS. They are stylesheets in which the properties for displaying a presenter are defined. Examples of properties are colors, width, height, and font. As a general principle, it is better to use styles instead of fixed constraints, because your application will be more responsive.

Note, however, that a stylesheet does not cover all aspects of a widget and you may need properties that are not covered in the current version of Spec. When moving to Toplo widgets in the future, Spec will revisit its style support and it will improve the coverage.

15.3 Stylesheets

Spec collects the style for a presenter, then collects the styles for its subpresenters.

Root level

A stylesheet always has a root element and this root element has to be called `.application`. The following stylesheet declares that the font for the application (i.e., for all the presenters if not redefined in another style) is 10 pixels and Source Sans Pro.

```
.application [
  Font { #name: "Source Sans Pro", #size: 10 },
  ...
```

Subpresenter

Each style follows a cascading style, starting from .application. Here are three styles:

```
.application.label.header
.application.link
.application.checkBox
```

15.4 Style declaration

Morphic styles are declared using STON. STON is a textual object notation. It is described in a dedicated chapter in the *Enterprise Pharo* book available at https://books.pharo.org.

Spec styles support five properties: Geometry, Draw, Font, Container, and Text, as shown by the following example.

```
Geometry { #hResizing: true }
Draw { #color:  Color { #red: 1, #green: 0, #blue: 0, #alpha: 1}}
Draw { #color: #blue}
Font { #name: "Lucida Grande", #size: 10, #bold: true }
Container { #borderColor: Color { #rgb: 0, #alpha: 0 },
    #borderWidth: 2,
    #padding: 5 }
```

You can define your style globally at the level of your application, and apply it to a specific presenter with the message addStyle:. For example aPresenter addStyle: 'section' selects the .section style and assigns it to the receiver.

15.5 Stylesheet examples

Here are two examples of stylesheets.

```
styleSheet

 ^ SpStyleVariableSTONReader fromString: '
  .application [
    Font { #name: "Source Sans Pro", #size: 10 },
    Geometry { #height: 25 },
    .label [
      Geometry { #hResizing: true },
      .headerError [Draw { #color:  Color{ #red: 1, #green: 0, #blue: 0, #alpha: 1}} ],
      .headerSuccess [Draw { #color:  Color{ #red: 0, #green: 1, #blue: 0, #alpha: 1}} ],
```

```
    .header [
      Draw { #color: Color{ #rgb: 622413393 }},
      Font { #name: "Lucida Grande", #size: 10, #bold: true } ],
    .shortcut [
      Draw { #color: Color{ #rgb: 622413393 } },
      Font { #name: "Lucida Grande", #size: 10 } ],
    .fixed [
      Geometry { #hResizing: false, #width: 100 } ],
    .dim [
      Draw { #color : Color{ #rgb: 708480675 } } ]
  ]'
```

The next one extends the default stylesheet that is returned by the expression SpStyle defaultStyleSheet.

```
styleSheet

  ^ SpStyle defaultStyleSheet, (SpStyleVariableSTONReader fromString: '
  .application [
    Draw { #backgroundColor: #lightRed},
    .section [
      Draw { #color: #green, #backgroundColor: #lightYellow},
      Font {  #name: "Verdana", #size: 12, #italic: true, #bold: true}],
    .disabled [ Draw { #backgroundColor: #lightGreen} ],
    .textInputField [ Draw { #backgroundColor: #blue} ],
    .label [
      Font {  #name: "Verdana", #size: 10, #italic: false, #bold: true},
      Draw { #color: #red, #backgroundColor: #lightBlue} ]
  ]')
```

15.6 Anatomy of a style

Each style element kind uses specific properties defined by its associated classes which subclass SpPropertyStyle. SpPropertyStyle has 5 subclasses: SpContainerStyle, SpDrawStyle, SpFontStyle, SpTextStyle, and SpGeometryStyle.

These subclasses define the 5 types of properties that exist.

- Container: SpContainerStyle - It manages the alignment of the presenters. Usually the style is set by the parent presenter, which is the one that contains and arranges the subpresenters.

- Draw: SpDrawStyle - It modifies the properties related to the drawing of the presenter, such as the color and the background color.

- Font: `SpFontStyle` - It defines properties related to fonts.
- Text: `SpTextStyle` - It controls the properties of the `SpTextInputFieldPresenter`.
- Geometry: `SpGeometryStyle` - It defines sizes, like width, height, minimum height, etc.

If you want to be sure that you browse the adequate class, just send the message `stonName` to the class. It will return the string used in the STON notation. For example, `SpDrawStyle stonName` returns `Draw`.

Example

If we want to change the color of a presenter, we need to create a string and use the `SpDrawStyle` property. For setting the color, we can use either the hexadecimal code of the color, or a method selector of the `Color` class.

Here we define two styles: `lightGreen` and `lightBlue` that can be applied to any presenter.

```
'.application [
  .lightGreen [ Draw { #color: #B3E6B5 } ],
  .lightBlue [ Draw { #color: #lightBlue } ] ]'
```

15.7 Environment variables

We can also use environment variables to get the values of the predefined colors and fonts of the current UI theme. For example, we can create two styles for changing the font of the text and one for the background color of a presenter:

```
'.application [
  .codeFont [ Font { #name: EnvironmentFont(#code) } ],
  .textFont [ Font { #name: EnvironmentFont(#default) } ],
  .bg [ Draw { #color: EnvironmentColor(#background) } ]
]'
```

Check the subclasses of `SpStyleEnvironmentVariable`.

15.8 Top-level changes

We can change the styles for all the presenters. For instance, we can display all the text in bold by default with this style:

```
'.application [
    Font { #bold: true }
]'
```

15.9 Defining an application and its style

Suppose we like to style the Mail Application we introduced in Chapter 12 and extend in Chapter 13. Let's say that we like the labels in the mail editing part of the UI to use a bigger font and a blue color. Furthermore, let's say that we like to use a light yellow background for fields and that we want a black border around the field to edit the body of a mail. That brings us to this stylesheet:

```
'.application [
    .fieldLabel [ Font { #size: 12 }, Draw { #color: #blue } ],
    .field [ Draw { #backgroundColor: #lightYellow } ],
    .bodyField [ Container { #borderWidth: 1, #borderColor: #black} ]
]'
```

The style `.fieldLabel` defines a 12-pixel blue font. The style `.field` defines a light yellow background color. The style `.bodyField` defines a black 1-pixel border.

To use styles, we need to associate the main presenter with an application. One way of achieving that would be this way:

```
| mailClient application styleSheet |
mailClient := MailClientPresenter on: MailAccount new.
application := SpApplication new.
mailClient application: application.

styleSheet := SpStyle defaultStyleSheet,
    (SpStyleVariableSTONReader fromString:
    '.application [
        .fieldLabel [ Font { #size: 12 }, Draw { #color: #blue } ],
        .field [ Draw { #backgroundColor: #lightYellow } ],
        .bodyField [ Container { #borderWidth: 1, #borderColor: #black } ]
    ]').

app styleSheet: SpStyle defaultStyleSheet , styleSheet.
```

But this way of working requires creating the stylesheet outside the context of the Mail Application. Instead, we will introduce a new application class and we override the method `styleSheet`.

```
SpApplication << #MailClientApplication
    slots: {};
    package: 'CodeOfSpec20Book'
```

```
MailClientApplication >> styleSheet

    | customStyleSheet |
    customStyleSheet := SpStyleVariableSTONReader fromString:
      '.application [
        .fieldLabel [ Font { #size: 12 }, Draw { #color: #blue } ],
        .field [ Draw { #backgroundColor: #lightYellow } ],
        .bodyField [ Container { #borderWidth: 1, #borderColor: #black }
      ]
      ]'.
    ^ super styleSheet , customStyleSheet
```

Note that this method includes a super send. `SpApplication >> styleSheet` answers the default stylesheet, which is the same as `SpStyle defaultStyleSheet` that we saw before. By combining the default stylesheet and our own stylesheet with the , message, we ensure that all the default styles for all presenters are still applied, and our styles are applied on top of the default styles.

To open the Mail Application easily, we define the `start` method:

```
MailClientApplication >> start

    (MailClientPresenter on: MailAccount new)
      application: self;
      open
```

With this code in place, we can open the Mail Application with:

```
MailClientApplication new start
```

Of course, that would not have much effect. After all, we did not apply the styles yet.

15.10 Applying styles

The styles we defined in the previous section were intended for the `EmailPresenter` class, which defines a form-like UI to edit a mail. The original implementation of `defaultLayout` was:

```
EmailPresenter >> defaultLayout

    | toLine subjectLine fromLine |
    fromLine := SpBoxLayout newTopToBottom
      add: 'From:' expand: false;
      add: from expand: false;
      yourself.
    toLine := SpBoxLayout newTopToBottom
      add: 'To:' expand: false;
```

Styling applications

```
    add: to expand: false;
    yourself.
  subjectLine := SpBoxLayout newTopToBottom
    add: 'Subject:' expand: false;
    add: subject expand: false;
    yourself.
  ^ SpBoxLayout newTopToBottom
    spacing: 10;
    add: fromLine expand: false;
    add: toLine expand: false;
    add: subjectLine expand: false;
    add: body;
    yourself
```

To style the fields, we have to make some changes. The implementation above is based on the method add:expand: which, out of convenience, allows the first argument to be a string, e.g. add: 'From:' expand: false. We cannot style a string. We can only style presenters, so we have to create the label presenters ourselves. Then we can add the required styles to the three label presenters by sending addStyle: 'fieldLabel'. Note that the definition of the style uses .fieldLabel. When sending the message addStyle:, the leading period is omitted in the argument string representing the style.

```
EmailPresenter >> defaultLayout

  | toLine subjectLine fromLine fromLabel toLabel subjectLabel |
  fromLabel := self newLabel
    label: 'From:';
    addStyle: 'fieldLabel';
    yourself.
  fromLine := SpBoxLayout newTopToBottom
    add: fromLabel expand: false;
    add: from expand: false;
    yourself.
  toLabel := self newLabel
    label: 'To:';
    addStyle: 'fieldLabel';
    yourself.
  toLine := SpBoxLayout newTopToBottom
    add: toLabel expand: false;
    add: to expand: false;
    yourself.
  subjectLabel := self newLabel
    label: 'Subject:';
    addStyle: 'fieldLabel';
    yourself.
  subjectLine := SpBoxLayout newTopToBottom
```

15.11 Dynamically applying styles

```
    add: subjectLabel expand: false;
    add: subject expand: false;
    yourself.
  ^ SpBoxLayout newTopToBottom
      spacing: 10;
      add: fromLine expand: false;
      add: toLine expand: false;
      add: subjectLine expand: false;
      add: body;
      yourself
```

Now that the labels are styled, the next step is to style the fields. We adapt the method `initializePresenters`, where they are initialized. Originally, the method included the first four statements. We add four more to add the styles.

```
EmailPresenter >> initializePresenters

  from := self newTextInput.
  to := self newTextInput.
  subject := self newTextInput.
  body := self newText.
  from addStyle: 'field'.
  to addStyle: 'field'.
  subject addStyle: 'field'.
  body addStyle: 'field'; addStyle: 'bodyField'
```

While we add one style for the `from`, `to`, and `subject` presenters, we add two styles to the `body` presenter. The `field` style will apply the background color. The `bodyField` style will apply the black border.

With `MailClientApplication new start` we can open the Mail Application and see styling in action. Figure 15-1 shows the window.

15.11 Dynamically applying styles

Suppose that we like to see a different background color for the fields if the edited mail is a draft mail. That is where dynamic styling comes in.

We can add and remove styles at runtime when the state of the application changes. Let's do that for the styles of the fields.

First, we adapt the method `styleSheet` of our application class to add new styles. We add the style `.draftMail` with a nested style `.field` that specifies a pink background color. The nesting expresses that the `.field` style applies in the context of the `.draftMail` style.

Styling applications

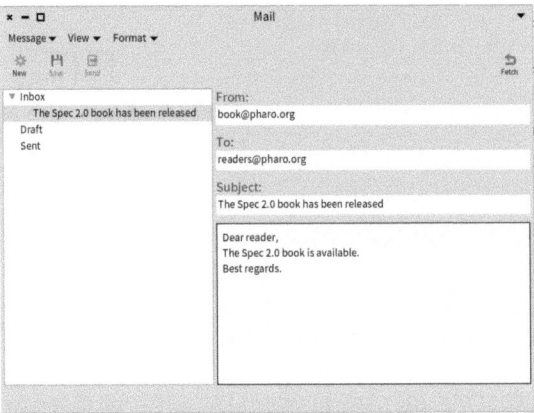

Figure 15-1 The stylesheet has been applied to the label and the fields.

```
MailClientApplication >> styleSheet

  | customStyleSheet |
  customStyleSheet := SpStyleVariableSTONReader fromString:
    '.application [
      .fieldLabel [ Font { #size: 12 }, Draw { #color: #blue } ],
      .field [ Draw { #backgroundColor: #lightYellow } ],
      .draftMail [
        .field [ Draw { #backgroundColor: #pink } ]
        ],
      .bodyField [ Container { #borderWidth: 1, #borderColor: #black }
    ]
    ]'.
  ^ super styleSheet , customStyleSheet
```

The next step is to apply the new style. EmailPresenter instances have a model. When it changes, the presenter is notified via the modelChanged method. The original implementation was:

```
EmailPresenter >> modelChanged

  from text: (self model from ifNil: [ '' ]).
  to text: (self model to ifNil: [ '' ]).
  subject text: (self model subject ifNil: [ '' ]).
  body text: (self model body ifNil: [ '' ])
```

We can easily extend it to apply different styles depending on the kind of model, which holds an instance of the Email class.

```
EmailPresenter >> modelChanged

    from text: (self model from ifNil: [ '' ]).
    to text: (self model to ifNil: [ '' ]).
    subject text: (self model subject ifNil: [ '' ]).
    body text: (self model body ifNil: [ '' ]).
    self model isDraft
        ifTrue: [
            from addStyle: 'draftMail.field'.
            to addStyle: 'draftMail.field'.
            subject addStyle: 'draftMail.field'.
            body addStyle: 'draftMail.field' ]
        ifFalse: [
            from removeStyle: 'draftMail.field'.
            to removeStyle: 'draftMail.field'.
            subject removeStyle: 'draftMail.field'.
            body removeStyle: 'draftMail.field' ]
```

Let's open the Mail Application again and select different kinds of mail. Figure 15-2 shows the two styles.

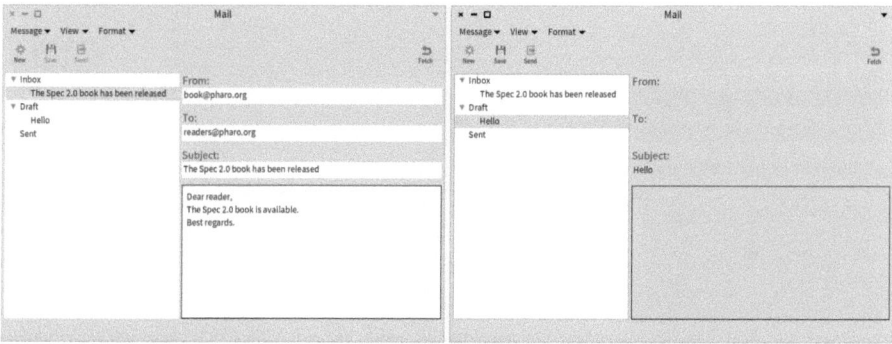

Figure 15-2 A different style for different kinds of mail.

15.12 Conclusion

Using styles in Spec is a nice feature. It makes it easier to have a consistent design as we can add the same style to several presenters. If we want to change some style, we only edit the stylesheet. We can dynamically change how a presenter looks.

CHAPTER **16**

Using Athens and Roassal in Spec

A part of this chapter was originally written by Renaud de Villemeur. We thank him for his contribution. It shows how you can integrate vector graphic drawing within Spec components. This chapter shows how you can use Athens (a canvas using Cairo as backend) to draw using a low-level API on a canvas inside a Spec presenter. It then shows how you can use Roassal (a visualization engine) within a Spec presenter. Finally we show how you can integrate into a Spec component a Morph that draws into a Athens canvas.

16.1 Introduction

There are two different computer graphics: vector and raster graphics. Raster graphics represent images as a collection of pixels. Vector graphics uses geometric primitives such as points, lines, curves, or polygons to represent images. These primitives are created using mathematical equations.

Both types of computer graphics have advantages and disadvantages. The advantages of vector graphics over raster are:

- smaller size,
- ability to zoom indefinitely,
- moving, scaling, filling, and rotating do not degrade the quality of an image.

Ultimately, pictures on a computer are displayed on a screen with a specific display dimension. However, while raster graphics doesn't scale very well when the resolution differs too much from the picture resolution, vector graphics are rasterized to fit the display they will appear on. Rasterization is taking an image described in a vector graphics format and transforming it into a set of pixels for output on a screen.

Morphic is using a raster approach. It converts the canvas contents into a pixel based structure (the class Form). Most graphics in Pharo are raster graphics: Form the low-level abstraction is used by Morphic. Pharo, however, offers a vector graphics alternative. For this, it uses and exposes Cairo to the user. Two APIs are available:

- the older one, called Athens, is protecting more the developers from possible mistakes.
- Alexandrie is a new and more low-level API. It has been more aggressively optimized. It is the foundation for Bloc the replacement of Morphic.

When you integrate Athens with Spec, you'll use its rendering engine to create your picture. It is transformed into a Form and displayed on the screen.

16.2 Direct integration of Athens with Spec

We first create a presenter named AthensExamplePresenter. This is the presenter that will support the actual rendering using Athens.

```
SpPresenter << #AthensExamplePresenter
    slots: { #athensPresenter };
    package: 'CodeOfSpec20Book'
```

We define a simple layout to place the athensPresenter.

```
AthensExamplePresenter >> defaultLayout

    ^ SpBoxLayout newTopToBottom
        add: athensPresenter;
        yourself
```

This presenter creates and configures an SpAthensPresenter instance as follows:

```
AthensExamplePresenter >> initializePresenters

    athensPresenter := self instantiate: SpAthensPresenter.
    athensPresenter surfaceExtent: 600@400.
    athensPresenter drawBlock: [ :canvas | self render: canvas ]
```

It configures the AthensPresenter to draw with the render: message. The render: method is a typical sequence of instructions to configure the canvas.

16.2 Direct integration of Athens with Spec

```
AthensExamplePresenter >> render: canvas
    | surface font |
    surface := canvas surface.
    font := LogicalFont familyName: 'Source Sans Pro' pointSize: 10.
    surface clear.
    canvas
        setPaint: ((LinearGradientPaint from: 0@0  to: surface extent)
        colorRamp: {  0 -> Color white. 1 -> Color black }).
    canvas drawShape: (0@0 extent: surface extent).
    canvas setFont: font.
    canvas setPaint: Color pink.
    canvas
        pathTransform translateX: 20 Y: 20 + (font getPreciseAscent);
        scaleBy: 2;
        rotateByDegrees: 25.
    canvas drawString: 'Hello Athens in Pharo/Morphic'
```

Executing `AthensExamplePresenter new open` produces Figure 16-1.

Figure 16-1   A Spec presenter using an `SpAthensPresenter`.

This example is simple because we did not cover the rendering that may have to be invalidated if something changes, but it shows the key aspect of the architecture. You can do the same using the Alexandrie new canvas based on Cairo. Notice that here we directly draw on the canvas without manipulating Morphic objects. This is what we will do in a following section.

207

16.3 Roassal Spec integration

In this section, we describe how you can define a Spec presenter that lets you draw Roassal visualisations.

Imagine that you want to draw using Roassal some shapes. Here we draw two boxes. But you can also draw paths and other graphical element.

```
| c blueBox redBox |
c := RSCanvas new.
blueBox := RSBox new
    size: 80;
    color: #blue.
redBox := RSBox new
    size: 80;
    color: #red.
c
    add: blueBox;
    add: redBox.
blueBox translateBy: 40 @ 20.
c
```

Using SpRoassalInspectorPresenter.

Building a Roassal supporting Spec presenter is as simple as creating an instance of SpRoassalInspectorPresenter and passing it the canvas on which we draw the Roassal visualization.

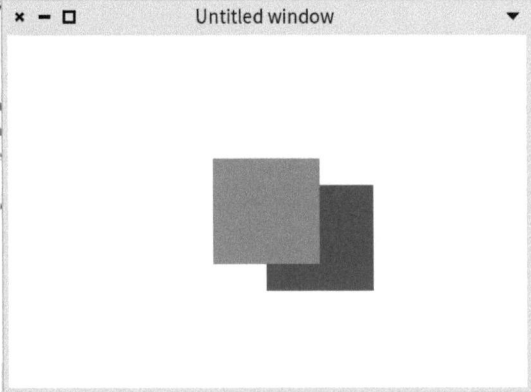

Figure 16-2 A Spec application with an Athens presenter.

This is what the following expression is doing SpRoassalInspectorPresenter new canvas: c; open

16.4 SpRoassalPresenter

Executing the following snippet should open a Spec window with a presenter inside as shown in Figure 16-2.

```
| c blueBox redBox |
c := RSCanvas new.
blueBox := RSBox new
    size: 80;
    color: #blue.
redBox := RSBox new
    size: 80;
    color: #red.
c
    add: blueBox;
    add: redBox.
blueBox translateBy: 40 @ 20.

SpRoassalInspectorPresenter new canvas: c; open
```

16.4 SpRoassalPresenter

Spec proposes a presenter dedicated to Roassal visualizations. Such a presenter is called `SpRoassalPresenter` and you can use it using the `newRoassal` message in an `initializePresenter` method. Here is how the `SpColorPicker` uses it.

```
SpColorPicker >> defaultLayout

    | sp sp2 |
    sp := self newRoassal.
    sp2 := self newPresenter.
    sp2 layout: SpBoxLayout newTopToBottom.
    sp canvas color: Color black translucent.

    ^ SpBoxLayout newTopToBottom
        add: colorMap height: 150;
        add: colorSlider height: 25;
        add: alphaSlider height: 25;
        add: colorCodePresenter expand: false;
        add: sp2 height: 10;
        add: sp height: 1;
        add: paletteChooser;
        spacing: 1;
        yourself.
```

The main API of `SpRoassalPresenter` are the method `canvas` and `script` as shown in the following test. You can interact with a Roassal canvas normally and the result gets displayed in the Roassal presenter.

```
testBasic
   | spec value window |
   self isValid ifFalse: [ ^ self ].
   spec := SpRoassalPresenter new.
   window := spec asWindow open.
   value := 0.

   spec script: [ :view | view addShape: RSBox new. value := value + 1
       ].
   self assert: value equals: 1.
   spec script: [ :view | view addShape: RSBox new. value := 0 ].
   self assert: value equals: 0.
   window close
```

16.5 Hello world in Athens via Morphic objects

The Pharo development team is actively working to replace Morphic by Bloc a new graphical stack. Still we believe that the following approach is worth documenting. We show how we can define a Morph that draws inside a athens canvas and how such a morph can be rendered inside a Spec component.

We show how to use Athens directly integrated with Morphic. This is why we create a `Morph` subclass. The expression `AthensHello new openInWindow` will display the same contents as the one of Figure 16-1.

First, we define a class which inherits from `Morph`:

```
Morph << #AthensHello
   slots: { #surface };
   package: 'CodeOfSpec20Book'
```

During the initialization phase, we create an Athens surface:

```
AthensHello >> initialize

   super initialize.
   self extent: self defaultExtent.
   surface := AthensCairoSurface extent: self extent
```

where `defaultExtent` is simply defined as

```
AthensHello >> defaultExtent

   ^ 400@400
```

The `drawOn:` method, mandatory in `Morph` subclasses, asks Athens to render its drawing and it will then display it in a Morphic canvas as a `Form` (a bitmap picture).

```
AthensHello >> drawOn: aCanvas

    self renderAthens.
    surface displayOnMorphicCanvas: aCanvas at: bounds origin
```

Our actual Athens code is located in the `renderAthens` method, and the result is stored in the `surface` instance variable.

```
AthensHello >> renderAthens

    | font |
    font := LogicalFont familyName: 'Arial' pointSize: 10.
    surface drawDuring: [ :canvas |
        surface clear.
        canvas setPaint: ((LinearGradientPaint from: 0@0  to: self extent)
            colorRamp: {  0 -> Color white. 1 -> Color black }).
        canvas drawShape: (0@0 extent: self extent).
        canvas setFont: font.
        canvas setPaint: Color pink.
        canvas pathTransform translateX: 20 Y: 20 + (font
        getPreciseAscent); scaleBy: 2; rotateByDegrees: 25.
        canvas drawString: 'Hello Athens in Pharo/Morphic' ]
```

Open the morph in a window with:

```
AthensHello new openInWindow
```

16.6 Handling resizing

You can create the window and see a nice gradient with a greeting text. You will notice, however, that when resizing the window, the Athens content is not resized. To fix this, we need one extra method.

```
AthensHello >> extent: aPoint

    | newExtent |
    newExtent := aPoint rounded.
    (bounds extent closeTo: newExtent) ifTrue: [ ^ self ].
    bounds := bounds topLeft extent: newExtent.
    surface := AthensCairoSurface extent: newExtent.
    self layoutChanged.
    self changed
```

Congratulations, you have now created your first morphic window whose contents is rendered using Athens. Now we show how to integrate this morph object into a Spec presenter.

16.7 Using the morph with Spec

Now that we have a morph, we can use it in a presenter, instance of the class `SpMorphPresenter`, as follows.

```
SpPresenter << #AthensHelloPresenter
    slots: { #morphPresenter };
    package: 'CodeOfSpec20Book'
```

We define a basic layout so that Spec knows where to place it.

```
AthensHelloPresenter >> defaultLayout

    ^ SpBoxLayout newTopToBottom
        add: morphPresenter;
        yourself
```

In `initializePresenters` we wrap the morph in a `SpMorphPresenter`.

```
AthensHelloPresenter >> initializePresenters

    morphPresenter := self instantiate: SpMorphPresenter.
    morphPresenter morph: AthensHello new
```

When we open the presenter it displays the morph:

```
AthensHelloPresenter new open
```

16.8 Conclusion

This chapter illustrated clearly that Spec can take advantage of canvas-related operations such as those proposed by Athens or Roassal to open the door to specific visuals.

CHAPTER 17

Customizing your Inspector

This chapter was originally written by Iona Thomas and we thank her for letting us use this material.

The Inspector is our favorite tool to look at and interact with objects. In Pharo, inspecting an object means opening this tool and interacting with your object. It is a key tool when developing in Pharo. It allows one to navigate the object structure, look at the state of the variables, change their value, or send messages. The inspector as most tools of the Pharo IDE is a tool written in Spec. In addition you can extend the Inspector to show information that is best suited for you. This is what we will see in this chapter.

17.1 Creating custom tabs

If you used the inspector a bit, you may have noticed that some objects have additional tabs showing up in the inspector. For example, both `Floats` and `Integers` have their first tabs showing different representations of numbers, as shown in Figure 17-1.

Another example is the `FileReference` class. When a file reference is inspected, according to the type of the file, different tabs show up with relevant information.

Creating a new tab is as simple as reusing existing Spec presenters or defining new ones for your specific case. For example, you can define a tab displaying a specific Roassal visualization.

The following sections explain how to add a few additional tabs to instances of `OrderedCollection`. This class already has a custom tab showing the list of its

Customizing your Inspector

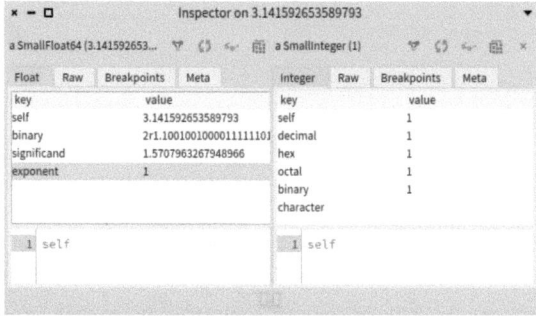

Figure 17-1 Inspecting numbers.

items which is defined by its superclass `Collection`.

17.2 Adding a tab with text

Let's add a first tab containing a text describing the first element of the collection. Define the following method:

```
OrderedCollection << inspectionFirstElement

  <inspectorPresentationOrder: 1 title: 'First Element'>

  ^ SpTextPresenter new
    text: 'The first element is ', self first asString;
    beNotEditable;
    yourself
```

Let us explain a bit the method definition

- `<inspectorPresentationOrder: 1 title: 'First Element'>` is a pragma that is detected when creating an inspector on an object. When creating an inspector on an instance of `OrderedCollection`, this method will be used to generate a tab. The title of the tab will be `First Element`, it will have position 1 in the order of tabs.

- The content of the tab is returned by the tagged method. Here we are creating a text presenter (`SpTextPresenter`) with the content we want and we specify that it should not be editable. This gives us the result shown in Figure 17-2.

Notice that our new tab is in the second position. This is because in `Collection<<inspectionItems:` (the method defining the Items tab) the order parameter is 0.

214

17.3 A tab with a table

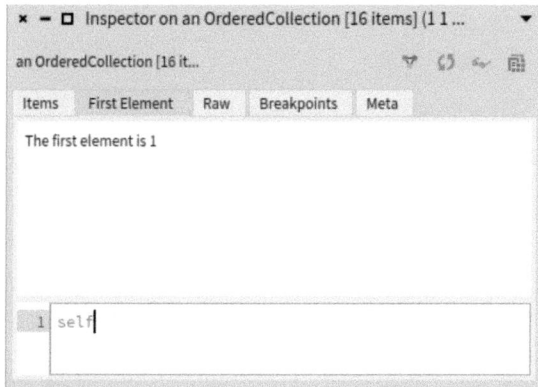

Figure 17-2 First element tab.

17.3 A tab with a table

Let's create a new tab that will display a table if the collection contains only numbers. It will show each number and the result of multiplying that number with 2.

First let's create the tab with the table:

```
OrderedCollection << inspectionMultipliedByTwo

  <inspectorPresentationOrder: 10 title: 'Multiply by 2'>

  | itemColumn multipliedByTwoColumn |
  itemColumn := SpStringTableColumn
    title: 'Item'
    evaluated: #yourself.
  itemColumn width: 30.
  multipliedByTwoColumn := SpStringTableColumn
    title: 'Multiply by 2'
    evaluated: [ :each | each * 2 ].
  ^ SpTablePresenter new
      addColumn: itemColumn;
      addColumn: multipliedByTwoColumn;
      items: self;
      beResizable;
      yourself
```

When we inspect a collection of numbers we see the tabs shown in Figure 17-3.

Customizing your Inspector

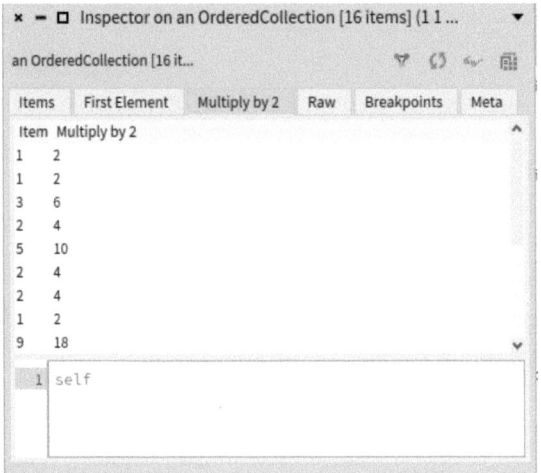

Figure 17-3 Multiplied by 2 tab.

17.4 Tab activation condition

If the collection contains elements that are not numbers, the tab crashes and looks like a red rectangle. By defining a method with the name xContext: (where x is the name of the method defining the tab) we can specify when we want to activate a given tab.

For example, the method defining the new tab is named inspectionMultipliedByTwo so the method defining the condition of the tab activation is named inspectionMultipliedByTwoContext:. We define it as follows:

```
OrderedCollection << inspectionMultipliedByTwoContext: aContext

  ^ aContext active: self containsOnlyNumbers
```
```
OrderedCollection << containsOnlyNumbers

  ^ self allSatisfy: [ :each | each isNumber ]
```

These two methods ensure that the tab is only displayed when there are only numbers in the collection.

17.5 Adding a raw view of a specific element of the collection

Sometimes you may want to provide addition tab but without any interpretation about the contents. This is what we call a raw view. For this we have to return an instance of StRawInspectionPresenter.

For example, adding a tab showing the raw view of the max value is expressed as follows:

```
OrderedCollection << inspectionMaxValue
    <inspectorPresentationOrder: 5 title: 'Max Value'>
    ^ StRawInspectionPresenter on: self max

OrderedCollection << inspectionMaxValueContext: aContext
    ^ aContext active: self containsOnlyIntegers
```

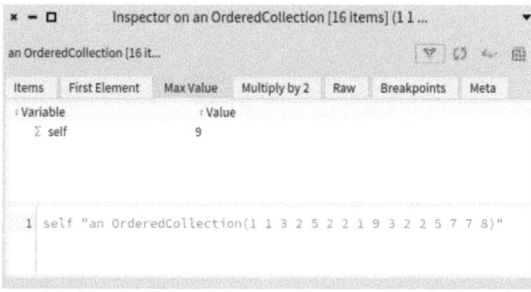

Figure 17-4 Inspect max value tab.

17.6 Removing the evaluator

As we can see in Figure 17-4, the self in the evaluator does not match the self in the max value, which is confusing. So we will hide the evaluator.

```
OrderedCollection << inspectionMaxValueContext: aContext
    aContext withoutEvaluator.
    ^ aContext active: self containsOnlyIntegers
```

By reinspecting the same collection we see the inspector in Figure 17-5.

Customizing your Inspector

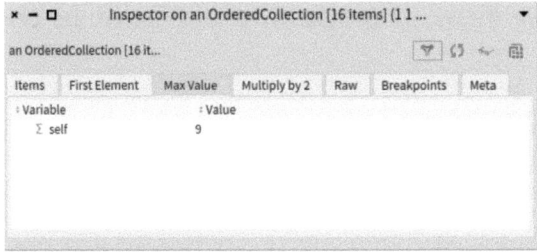

Figure 17-5 Removing the evaluator.

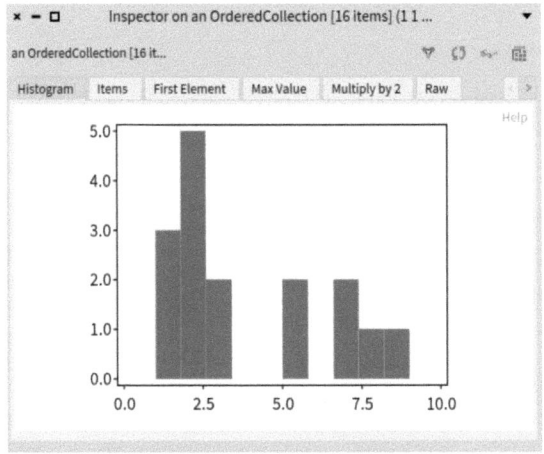

Figure 17-6 Histogram tab.

17.7 Adding Roassal charts

Roassal allows one to define visualizations. Such visualizations can also be added to the Inspector tabs. The library includes some common graphs like a histogram. Let's add a histogram of the values if there are only numbers in the collection. Roassal visualizations can be embedded in a presenter by sending the `asPresenter` message to an instance of `RSBuilder`. In the code below, `RSHistogramPlot` is a subclass of `RSBuilder`. You can also use a `SpRoassalPresenter` or `SPRoassalInspectorPresenter`.

```
OrderedCollection << inspectionIntegerHistogram

    <inspectorPresentationOrder: -1 title: 'Histogram'>
```

```
    | plot |
    plot := RSHistogramPlot new x: self.
    ^ plot asPresenter
```

```
OrderedCollection << inspectionIntegerHistogramContext: aContext

    aContext active: self containsOnlyIntegers.
    aContext withoutEvaluator.
```

By inspecting `{ 1 . 1 . 3 . 2 . 5 . 2. 2 . 1. 9. 3 . 2. 2. 5 . 7 . 7 . 8 } asOrderedCollection` we see the inspector shown in Figure 17-6.

17.8 Conclusion

In this chapter, we presented briefly how you can extend the Inspector adding specific tabs. This will shape the way you can see and interact with your objects. We presented how to define conditional tabs, as well as embed visualizations.

Part III

Working with Commands

CHAPTER 18

Commander: A powerful and simple command framework

Commander was a library originally developed by Denis Kudriashov. Commander 2.0 is the second iteration of that library. It was designed and developed by Julien Delplanque and Stéphane Ducasse. Note that Commander 2.0 is not compatible with Commander but it is really easy to migrate from Commander to Commander 2.0. We describe Commander 2.0 in the context of Spec. From now on, when we mention Commander we refer to Commander 2.0.

To explain the concepts, we will revisit the Mail Application that we introduced in Chapter 12 and extended in Chapter 13. You can load the code as explained in the first chapter of this book.

18.1 Commands

Commander models application actions as first-class objects following the Command design pattern. With Commander, you can express commands and use them to generate menus and toolbars, but also to script applications from the command line.

Every action is implemented as a separate command class (subclass of `CmCommand`) with an `execute` method and the state required for execution.

We will show later that for a UI framework, we need more information such as an icon and shortcut description. In addition, we will present how commands can be decorated with extra functionality in an extensible way.

223

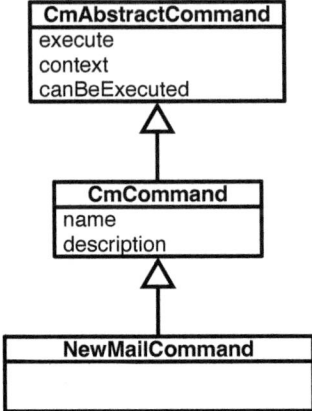

Figure 18-1 A simple command and its hierarchy.

18.2 Defining commands

A command is a simple object. It is an instance of a subclass of the class CmCommand. It has a description and a name. The name can be either static or dynamic as we will show later on. In addition, it has a context from which it extracts information to execute itself. In its basic form, there is no more than that.

Let us have a look at examples. We will define some commands for the Mail application and illustrate how they can be turned into menus, a menubar and a toolbar.

18.3 Adding a common superclass for the command classes

For convenience reasons, we define a common superclass of all the commands of the Mail application.

```
CmCommand << #MailClientCommand
    slots: {};
    package: 'CodeOfSpec20Book'
```

We define a simple helper method to make the code more readable:

```
MailClientCommand >> mailClientPresenter

    ^ self context
```

18.4 Adding the main commands

We implement subclasses of `MailClientCommand` to define the commands to create a new mail, to save a mail, to send a mail, to delete a mail, and to fetch mails.

NewMailCommand

```
MailClientCommand << #NewMailCommand
    slots: {};
    package: 'CodeOfSpec20Book'
```

In the `initialize` method, we set the name and the description.

```
NewMailCommand >> initialize

    super initialize.
    self
        name: 'New';
        description: 'Create a new email'
```

The `execute` method is the most important method of a command as it does the actual execution. We use the helper method `mailClientPresenter` that we defined in the superclass. The method sends the `newMail` message that we defined in Chapter 12.

```
NewMailCommand >> execute

    self mailClientPresenter newMail
```

In general, `execute` methods are simple, because they do not have enough knowledge about the state of the application to know what to do. Therefore they often delegate to the application.

As a general design advice, do not define application logic in a command. A command is just a representative of this behavior.

SaveMailCommand

```
MailClientCommand << SaveMailCommand
    slots: {};
    package: 'CodeOfSpec20Book'
```

```
SaveMailCommand >> initialize

    super initialize.
    self
        name: 'Save';
        description: 'Save the email'
```

```
SaveMailCommand >> execute

  self mailClientPresenter saveMail
```

```
SaveMailCommand >> canBeExecuted

  ^ self mailClientPresenter hasDraft
```

This command definition illustrates how we can control whether a command can be executed. The method `canBeExecuted` allows specifying such a condition.

In the previous command class, we did not implement `NewMailCommand >> canBeExecuted`, because creating a new mail is always possible and by default commands can be executed (`CmCommand >> canBeExecuted` answers `true`).

SendMailCommand

```
MailClientCommand << SendMailCommand
  slots: {};
  package: 'CodeOfSpec20Book'
```

```
SendMailCommand >> initialize

  super initialize.
  self
    name: 'Send';
    description: 'Send the selected email'
```

```
SendMailCommand >> execute

  self mailClientPresenter sendMail
```

```
SendMailCommand >> canBeExecuted

  ^ self mailClientPresenter hasDraft
```

DeleteMailCommand

```
MailClientCommand << DeleteMailCommand
  slots: {};
  package: 'CodeOfSpec20Book'
```

```
DeleteMailCommand >> initialize

  super initialize.
  self
    name: 'Delete';
    description: 'Delete the selected email'
```

```
DeleteMailCommand >> execute

    ^ self mailClientPresenter deleteMail

DeleteMailCommand >> canBeExecuted

    ^ self mailClientPresenter hasSelectedEmail
```

FetchMailCommand

```
MailClientCommand << FetchMailCommand
    slots: {};
    package: 'CodeOfSpec20Book'

FetchMailCommand >> initialize

    super initialize.
    self
        name: 'Fetch';
        description: 'Fetch email from the server'

FetchMailCommand >> execute

    self mailClientPresenter fetchMail
```

18.5 Adding placeholder commands

We also define placeholder commands for functionality that was not implemented by the Mail application in Chapter 12. We will not implement them here either. We only provide a name and a description, which are required for the UI.

FormatPlainTextCommand

```
MailClientCommand << FormatPlainTextCommand
    slots: {};
    package: 'CodeOfSpec20Book'

FormatPlainTextCommand >> initialize

    super initialize.
    self
        name: 'Plain text';
        description: 'Use plain text'
```

FormatRichTextCommand

```
MailClientCommand << FormatRichTextCommand
  slots: {};
  package: 'CodeOfSpec20Book'
```

```
FormatRichTextCommand >> initialize

  super initialize.
  self
    name: 'Rich text';
    description: 'Use rich text'
```

ShowCcFieldCommand

```
MailClientCommand << ShowCcFieldCommand
  slots: {};
  package: 'CodeOfSpec20Book'
```

```
ShowCcFieldCommand >> initialize

  super initialize.
  self
    name: 'Show CC field';
    description: 'Turn on the CC field'
```

ShowBccFieldCommand

```
MailClientCommand << ShowBccFieldCommand
  slots: {};
  package: 'CodeOfSpec20Book'
```

```
ShowCcFieldShowBccFieldCommandommand >> initialize

  super initialize.
  self
    name: 'Show BCC field';
    description: 'Turn on the BCC field'
```

18.6 Turning commands into menu items

Now that we have defined the commands, we would like to turn them into menus. In Spec, commands that are transformed into menu items are structured into a tree of command instances. The class method `buildCommandsGroupWith:forRoot:` of `SpPresenter` is a hook to let presenters define the root of the command instance tree.

The method `buildCommandsGroupWith:forRoot:` registers commands to which the presenter instance is passed as context. Note that here we just add plain commands, but we can also create groups. Later in this chapter we will also specify a menubar and a toolbar in this method. For now, we restrict it to the context menu for the `MailAccountPresenter`.

```
MailClientPresenter class >>
  buildCommandsGroupWith: presenter
  forRoot: rootCommandGroup

  rootCommandGroup
    register: (self buildAccountMenuWith: presenter)
```

The method above delegates to `MailClientPresenter class >> buildAccountMenuWith:`, which adds the delete and the send commands. The method answers a CmCommandGroup instance with a name 'AccountMenu'. The name will not be visible in the UI because we send beRoot. A command is transformed into a command for Spec using the message forSpec.

```
MailClientPresenter class >> buildAccountMenuWith: presenter

  ^ (CmCommandGroup named: 'AccountMenu') asSpecGroup
      beRoot;
      register: (DeleteMailCommand forSpec context: presenter);
      register: (SendMailCommand forSpec context: presenter);
      yourself
```

18.7 Using fillWith:

In Chapter 12, we defined the method `MailClientPresenter >> accountMenu` to return the context menu for the `MailAccountPresenter`. When using commands, we implement it differently. We create a new menu and fill it with the commands defined in the method above. A presenter has access to the root of the command tree through the message `rootCommandsGroup`. Subtrees can be accessed by sending the / message. By using commands, building up the context menu is almost trivial:

```
MailClientPresenter >> accountMenu

  ^ self newMenu
      fillWith: (self rootCommandsGroup / 'AccountMenu');
      yourself
```

When reopening the interface with:

```
(MailClientPresenter on: MailAccount new) open
```

you should see the menu items as shown in Figure 18-2. As we will show later, we could even replace a menu item with another one, changing its name, or icon in place.

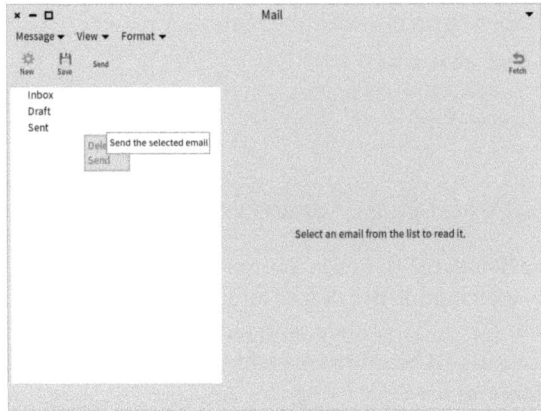

Figure 18-2   Two menu items with the mouse pointing at the second item.

18.8 Managing icons and shortcuts

By default a command does not know about Spec-specific behavior, because a command does not have to be linked to UI. Obviously you want to have icons and shortcut bindings when you are designing an interactive application.

Commander supports the addition of icons and shortcut keys to commands. Let's see how it works from a user perspective. The framework offers two methods to set an icon and a shortcut key: iconName: and shortcutKey:. We can specialize the method asSpecCommand as follows:

```
NewMailCommand >> asSpecCommand

    ^ super asSpecCommand
        iconName: #smallNew;
        shortcutKey: $n meta;
        yourself
```

```
SaveMailCommand >> asSpecCommand

    ^ super asSpecCommand
        iconName: #smallSave;
        shortcutKey: $s meta;
        yourself
```

18.9 Managing a menubar

```
SendMailCommand >> asSpecCommand

    ^ super asSpecCommand
        iconName: #smallExport;
        shortcutKey: $l meta;
        yourself

DeleteMailCommand >> asSpecCommand

    ^ super asSpecCommand
        shortcutKey: $d meta;
        yourself

FetchMailCommand >> asSpecCommand

    ^ super asSpecCommand
        iconName: #refresh;
        shortcutKey: $f meta;
        yourself
```

Remember that commands are created using the message `forSpec`. This message takes care of the calling `asSpecCommand`.

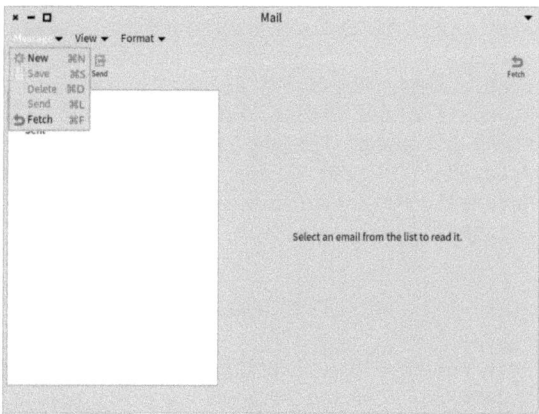

Figure 18-3 With a menubar.

18.9 Managing a menubar

Commander also supports menubar creation as shown in Figure 18-3. The logic is the same as for contextual menus: we define a group and register it under a given root, and we tell the presenter to use this group as a menubar.

First, we have to define the menubar. We extend the method we defined before:

```
MailClientPresenter class >>
  buildCommandsGroupWith: presenter
  forRoot: rootCommandGroup

  rootCommandGroup
    register: (self buildAccountMenuWith: presenter);
    register: (self buildMenuBarGroupWith: presenter)
```

The method delegates to `MailClientPresenter >> buildMenuBarGroupWith:`:

```
MailClientPresenter class >> buildMenuBarGroupWith: presenter

  ^ (CmCommandGroup named: 'MenuBar') asSpecGroup
    beRoot;
    register: (self buildMessageMenuWith: presenter);
    register: (self buildViewMenuWith: presenter);
    register: (self buildFormatMenuWith: presenter);
    yourself
```

In its turn, this method delegates to three other methods:

```
MailClientPresenter class >> buildMessageMenuWith: presenter

  ^ (CmCommandGroup named: 'Message') asSpecGroup
    register: (NewMailCommand forSpec context: presenter);
    register: (SaveMailCommand forSpec context: presenter);
    register: (DeleteMailCommand forSpec context: presenter);
    register: (SendMailCommand forSpec context: presenter);
    register: (FetchMailCommand forSpec context: presenter);
    yourself
```

```
MailClientPresenter class >> buildViewMenuWith: presenter

  ^ (CmCommandGroup named: 'View') asSpecGroup
    register: (ShowCcFieldCommand forSpec context: presenter);
    register: (ShowBccFieldCommand forSpec context: presenter);
    yourself
```

```
MailClientPresenter >> buildFormatMenuWith: presenter

  ^ (CmCommandGroup named: 'Format') asSpecGroup
    register: (FormatPlainTextCommand forSpec context: presenter);
    register: (FormatRichTextCommand forSpec context: presenter);
    yourself
```

Now that the command tree for the menubar is defined, we can use it. In Chapter 12, we defined `MailClientPresenter >> #initializeMenuBar`. We can replace it by:

```
MailClientPresenter >> initializeMenuBar

    menuBar := self newMenuBar.
    menuBar fillWith: self rootCommandsGroup / 'MenuBar'
```

Figure 18-3 shows the result of adding the menubar based on commands.

18.10 Introducing groups

As you can see in Figure 18-3, the first menu in the menubar shows a plain list of menu items. That was not the case when we implemented the first version of the Mail Application. In Chapter 13, Figure 13-2 shows a menu with two groups. The first four menu items where separated from the fifth menu item with a separator line.

We can achieve the same grouping with commands. Commands can be managed in groups and such groups can be turned into corresponding menu item sections.

Let's make the required changes to the method `MailClientPresenter class >> #buildMessageMenuWith:` that we introduced before.

```
MailClientPresenter class >> buildMessageMenuWith: presenter

    | fetchGroup |
    fetchGroup := CmCommandGroup new asSpecGroup
        register: (FetchMailCommand forSpec context: presenter);
        beDisplayedAsGroup;
        yourself.
    ^ (CmCommandGroup named: 'Message') asSpecGroup
        register: (NewMailCommand forSpec context: presenter);
        register: (SaveMailCommand forSpec context: presenter);
        register: (DeleteMailCommand forSpec context: presenter);
        register: (SendMailCommand forSpec context: presenter);
        register: fetchGroup;
        yourself
```

We already used groups for the different menus in the menubar. In this method, we had a group named "Message". The name was also the label of the menu in the menubar. Instead of registering the `FetchMailCommand` as the last command in the menu, we register a new group, which is defined at the beginning of the method. The new group has no name, because we do not need one, and holds only one command, the `FetchMailCommand`.

An important message is `beDisplayedAsGroup`. It indicates that in a menu, the new group should be separated from the other menu items, instead of being added as a menu item with a nested menu. Figure 18-4 shows what the menu would look like if beDisplayedAsGroup is not sent. In situations where nested menus are desired, that would be fine, but giving the group a nice name would be preferable, as "Unnamed group" is the default name.

Figure 18-4   Nested menu with the mouse pointing at its name.

In our case, we do not want a nested menu. We want a separate section in the menu. With the implementation of `MailClientPresenter class >> #buildMessageMenuWith:` above, we see a menu as shown in Figure 18-5. As in Chapter 13, now there are two groups of commands, separated by a line.

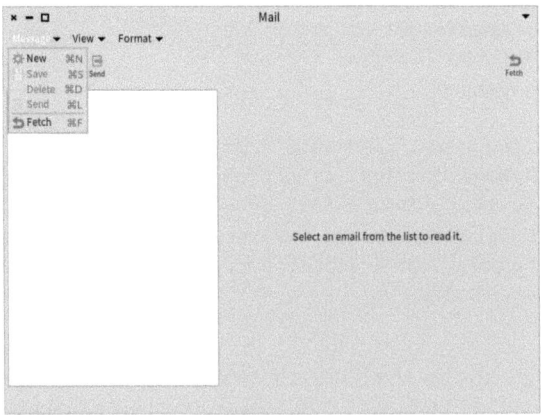

Figure 18-5   Menu with a separate group.

18.11 Extending menus

Building menus is nice, but sometimes we need to add a menu to an existing one. Commander supports this via a dedicated pragma, called `<extension-Commands>` that identifies extensions.

Imagine that we want to add new functionality to the Mail Application and that this behavior is packaged in another package, for instance `CodeOfSpec20Book-Extensions`. As an example, we will add the ability to create new mails from a template. To reduce the additional code for such functionality, we will keep things simple. It is not our intention to introduce a full-fledged templating system. We will restrict the feature to a template for the body of a mail.

Defining a new command

First, we will define a new command and second, we will show how we can extend the existing menubar with an extra menu. Adding menu items to existing menus and adding toolbar buttons to an existing toolbar can be done in a similar way.

```
MailClientCommand << #NewMailTemplateCommand
  slots: { #bodyTemplate };
  package: 'CodeOfSpec20Book-Extensions'
```

Note that we put the new command class in an extension package, while all the code so far resides in package "CodeOfSpec20Book".

One could imagine having template values for all attributes of a mail. As mentioned before, we keep thing simple. Only the body is a template. That is why there is only one instance variable. We will need a write accessor method to set the body template, so let's define it.

```
NewMailTemplateCommand >> bodyTemplate: aString

  bodyTemplate := aString
```

Later, the name of a template will be set as the name of the command, but we set a default in the `initialize` method:

```
NewMailTemplateCommand >> initialize

  super initialize.
  self
    name: 'New template';
    description: 'Create a new email from a template'
```

The `execute` method delegates the creation of a new mail to the `MailClient-Presenter`, similar to how we implemented `execute` methods of other command classes.

```
NewMailTemplateCommand >> execute

  self mailClientPresenter newFromTemplate: bodyTemplate
```

The implementation above requires the addition of an extension method to the `MailClientPresenter` class. The method below resides in the package "CodeOfSpec20Book-Extensions". The implementation of the method is similar to `MailClientPresenter >> newMail`. The only difference is setting the given template by sending the `body:` message to the new mail.

```
NewMailTemplateCommand >> newFromTemplate: aString

  editedEmail := Email new.
  editedEmail beDraft.
  editedEmail body: aString.
  reader updateLayoutForEmail: editedEmail.
  self modelChanged
```

18.12 Declaring extension

The last missing piece is the declaration of the extension of the commands with the pragma `<extensionCommands>` on the class side of the `MailClientPresenter` class as follows:

```
MailClientPresenter class >>
  buildTemplateCommandsGroupWith: presenter
  forRoot: rootCommandGroup

  <extensionCommands>

  (rootCommandGroup / 'MenuBar')
    register: (self buildTemplateMenuWith: presenter)
```

This method resides in the package "CodeOfSpec20Book-Extensions". As we did before, this method uses another method to create the command tree for the new menu. That method resides in the package "CodeOfSpec20Book-Extensions" too. For our example, this method creates only two commands. In an extended implementation, one could imagine that the templates are objects and that they come from elsewhere.

Note the difference with the way we created commands before. Here, we do not send `forSpec` to the command class. Actually, we can't, because the commands have to be initialized with the body template. Therefore we create and initialize the commands, and send `asSpecCommand` to them. When registering them, we set the context.

18.13 Managing a toolbar

```
MailClientPresenter class >> buildTemplateMenuWith: presenter

  | letterTemplateCommand invitationTemplateCommand |
  invitationTemplateCommand := NewMailTemplateCommand new
    name: 'Invitation';
    bodyTemplate: 'Hi, you are invited to my party on <date>.';
    asSpecCommand.
  letterTemplateCommand := NewMailTemplateCommand new
    name: 'Letter';
    bodyTemplate: 'Dear <name>, I write you to inform you about
    <something>.';
    asSpecCommand.
  ^ (CmCommandGroup named: 'Templates') asSpecGroup
    register: (invitationTemplateCommand context: presenter);
    register: (letterTemplateCommand context: presenter);
    yourself
```

It is time to open the Mail Application again. Figure 18-6 shows the result with the "Templates" menu open. After selecting "Invitation" from the "Templates" menu, the new mail appears in the UI, as shown in Figure 18-7.

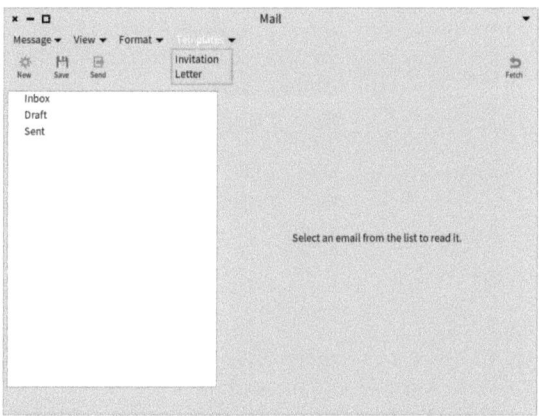

Figure 18-6 With menubar extension.

18.13 Managing a toolbar

We described how to use commands for context menus and for menubars. We can also use commands for toolbars. The big difference between menus and toolbars is that menu items are displayed only on demand. They show up after opening a menu. Toolbar buttons, on the other hand, are always visible. The constant visibility has an impact on the way button enablement has to be

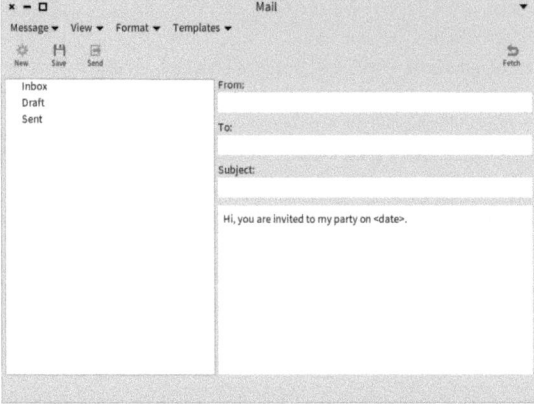

Figure 18-7 After creating a new mail from a template.

applied. For menu items, their enabled or disabled state is determined at the time of displaying them. For toolbar buttons, we will have to enable and disable them at the time the state of the application changes. We will discuss that soon. Let's first put a toolbar together based on commands. We know the pattern for menus. It is the same for toolbars.

The first step is to define the commands that will be available in the toolbar. We will adapt this method for the last time:

```
MailClientPresenter class >>
  buildCommandsGroupWith: presenter
  forRoot: rootCommandGroup

  rootCommandGroup
    register: (self buildAccountMenuWith: presenter);
    register: (self buildMenuBarGroupWith: presenter);
    register: (self buildToolBarGroupWith: presenter)
```

The last registration adds the commands for the toolbar. This is the implementation:

```
MailClientPresenter class >> buildToolBarGroupWith: presenter

  ^ (CmCommandGroup named: 'ToolBar') asSpecGroup
    beRoot;
    register: (NewMailCommand forSpec context: presenter);
    register: (SaveMailCommand forSpec context: presenter);
    register: (SendMailCommand forSpec context: presenter);
    register: (FetchMailCommand forSpec context: presenter);
    yourself
```

18.13 Managing a toolbar

This is very similar to how we defined the commands for the menus. Here we add the four commands that we like to include in the toolbar.

The next step is to fill the toolbar with these commands. To achieve that, we can change the method that we implemented before:

```
MailClientPresenter >> initializeToolBar

    toolBar := self newToolbar.
    toolBar fillWith: self rootCommandsGroup / 'ToolBar'
```

As you can see, we use the same pattern as `MailClientPresenter >> accountMenu` and `MailClientPresenter >> initializeMenuBar`. We create a new toolbar, and then send the message `fillWith:` to populate the toolbar with the commands coming from the command tree.

When we open the `MailClientPresenter` again, we see the toolbar as shown in Figure 18-8. All the toolbar buttons are positioned at the left side of the toolbar. That is different from the toolbar shown in Figure 13-3 in Chapter 13, where the button to fetch mail is positioned at the right side of the toolbar.

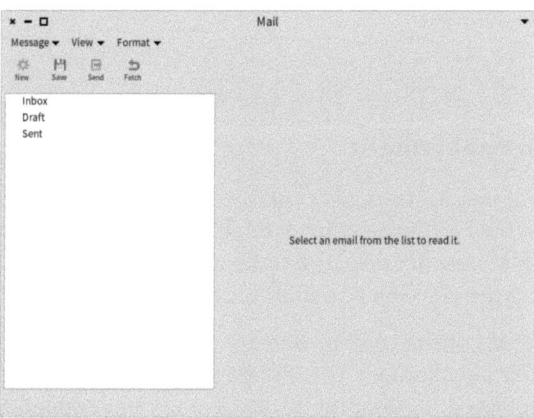

Figure 18-8 With a toolbar.

To position the button to fetch mail on the right side, we need an additional change in `FetchMailCommand >> asSpecCommand`. We send `beDisplayedOnRightSide`.

```
FetchMailCommand >> asSpecCommand

    ^ super asSpecCommand
        iconName: #refresh;
        shortcutKey: $f meta;
        beDisplayedOnRightSide;
```

yourself

When we open the presenter again, we see a toolbar as shown in Figure 18-9. The button to fetch mail is positioned on the right side.

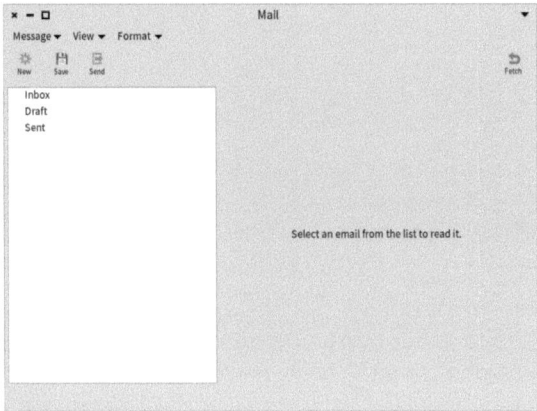

Figure 18-9 With a toolbar.

Toolbar button enablement

In the beginning of this section, we explained why enablement of toolbar buttons has to be handled differently from enablement of menu items. In the current state of the Mail Application, the toolbar buttons are always enabled. That is not desired, because clicking a toolbar button may lead to errors in the code.

The enablement state of the toolbar buttons should be updated every time the state of the application changes. For instance, sending a mail is possible only if a mail has been selected. In Chapter 13, we already introduced a method `MailClientPresenter >> updateToolBarButtons` to update the toolbar buttons. We can adapt it to update the enablement state of the toolbar buttons. However, Spec does not provide a method to refresh the toolbar buttons. The only way is to refill the toolbar. We can send the message `SpToolbarPresenter >> fillWith:` to achieve that, because that method empties the toolbar before filling it again.

```
MailClientPresenter >> updateToolBarButtons

  toolBar fillWith: self rootCommandsGroup / 'ToolBar'
```

And now that we have this method, we can remove the duplication in `MailClientPresenter >> initializeToolBar`.

```
MailClientPresenter >> initializeToolBar

    toolBar := self newToolbar.
    self updateToolBarButtons
```

18.14 Conclusion

In this chapter, we saw how you can define a command tree and populate it with subtrees for commands for particular contexts. Based on those subtrees, context menus, menubars and toolbars can be created with only a few lines of code. You learned how commands can be reused and customized. We presented groups of commands as a way to structure menus.